T0210620

Query Processing over Incomplete Databases

Synthesis Lectures on Data Management

Editor
H.V. Jagadish, *University of Michigan*

Founding Editor
M. Tamer Özsu, *University of Waterloo*

Synthesis Lectures on Data Management is edited by H.V. Jagadish of the University of Michigan. The series publishes 80–150 page publications on topics pertaining to data management. Topics include query languages, database system architectures, transaction management, data warehousing, XML and databases, data stream systems, wide scale data distribution, multimedia data management, data mining, and related subjects.

Query Processing over Incomplete Databases
Yunjun Gao and Xiaoye Miao
2018

On Uncertain Graphs
Arijit Khan, Yuan Ye, and Lei Chen
2018

Answering Queries Using Views
Foto Afrati and Rada Chirkova
2017

Databases on Modern Hardware: How to Stop Underutilization and Love Multicores
Anatasia Ailamaki, Erieta Liarou, Pınar Tözün, Danica Porobic, and Iraklis Psaroudakis
2017

Instant Recovery with Write-Ahead Logging: Page Repair, System Restart, Media Restore, and System Failover, Second Edition
Goetz Graefe, Wey Guy, and Caetano Sauer
2016

Generating Plans from Proofs: The Interpolation-based Approach to Query Reformulation
Michael Benedikt, Julien Leblay, Balder ten Cate, and Efthymia Tsamoura
2016

Veracity of Data: From Truth Discovery Computation Algorithms to Models of
Misinformation Dynamics
Laure Berti-Équille and Javier Borge-Holthoefer
2015

Datalog and Logic Databases
Sergio Greco and Cristina Molinaro
2015

Big Data Integration
Xin Luna Dong and Divesh Srivastava
2015

Instant Recovery with Write-Ahead Logging: Page Repair, System Restart, and Media
Restore
Goetz Graefe, Wey Guy, and Caetano Sauer
2014

Similarity Joins in Relational Database Systems
Nikolaus Augsten and Michael H. Böhlen
2013

Information and Influence Propagation in Social Networks
Wei Chen, Laks V.S. Lakshmanan, and Carlos Castillo
2013

Data Cleaning: A Practical Perspective
Venkatesh Ganti and Anish Das Sarma
2013

Data Processing on FPGAs
Jens Teubner and Louis Woods
2013

Perspectives on Business Intelligence
Raymond T. Ng, Patricia C. Arocena, Denilson Barbosa, Giuseppe Carenini, Luiz Gomes, Jr.,
Stephan Jou, Rock Anthony Leung, Evangelos Milios, Renée J. Miller, John Mylopoulos, Rachel
A. Pottinger, Frank Tompa, and Eric Yu
2013

Semantics Empowered Web 3.0: Managing Enterprise, Social, Sensor, and Cloud-based
Data and Services for Advanced Applications
Amit Sheth and Krishnaprasad Thirunarayan
2012

Data Management in the Cloud: Challenges and Opportunities
Divyakant Agrawal, Sudipto Das, and Amr El Abbadi
2012

Query Processing over Uncertain Databases
Lei Chen and Xiang Lian
2012

Foundations of Data Quality Management
Wenfei Fan and Floris Geerts
2012

Incomplete Data and Data Dependencies in Relational Databases
Sergio Greco, Cristian Molinaro, and Francesca Spezzano
2012

Business Processes: A Database Perspective
Daniel Deutch and Tova Milo
2012

Data Protection from Insider Threats
Elisa Bertino
2012

Deep Web Query Interface Understanding and Integration
Eduard C. Dragut, Weiyi Meng, and Clement T. Yu
2012

P2P Techniques for Decentralized Applications
Esther Pacitti, Reza Akbarinia, and Manal El-Dick
2012

Query Answer Authentication
HweeHwa Pang and Kian-Lee Tan
2012

Declarative Networking
Boon Thau Loo and Wenchao Zhou
2012

Full-Text (Substring) Indexes in External Memory
Marina Barsky, Ulrike Stege, and Alex Thomo
2011

Spatial Data Management
Nikos Mamoulis
2011

Database Repairing and Consistent Query Answering
Leopoldo Bertossi
2011

Managing Event Information: Modeling, Retrieval, and Applications
Amarnath Gupta and Ramesh Jain
2011

Fundamentals of Physical Design and Query Compilation
David Toman and Grant Weddell
2011

Methods for Mining and Summarizing Text Conversations
Giuseppe Carenini, Gabriel Murray, and Raymond Ng
2011

Probabilistic Databases
Dan Suciu, Dan Olteanu, Christopher Ré, and Christoph Koch
2011

Peer-to-Peer Data Management
Karl Aberer
2011

Probabilistic Ranking Techniques in Relational Databases
Ihab F. Ilyas and Mohamed A. Soliman
2011

Uncertain Schema Matching
Avigdor Gal
2011

Fundamentals of Object Databases: Object-Oriented and Object-Relational Design
Suzanne W. Dietrich and Susan D. Urban
2010

Advanced Metasearch Engine Technology
Weiyi Meng and Clement T. Yu
2010

Web Page Recommendation Models: Theory and Algorithms
Sule Gündüz-Ögüdücü
2010

Multidimensional Databases and Data Warehousing
Christian S. Jensen, Torben Bach Pedersen, and Christian Thomsen
2010

Database Replication
Bettina Kemme, Ricardo Jimenez-Peris, and Marta Patino-Martinez
2010

Relational and XML Data Exchange
Marcelo Arenas, Pablo Barcelo, Leonid Libkin, and Filip Murlak
2010

User-Centered Data Management
Tiziana Catarci, Alan Dix, Stephen Kimani, and Giuseppe Santucci
2010

Data Stream Management
Lukasz Golab and M. Tamer Özsu
2010

Access Control in Data Management Systems
Elena Ferrari
2010

An Introduction to Duplicate Detection
Felix Naumann and Melanie Herschel
2010

Privacy-Preserving Data Publishing: An Overview
Raymond Chi-Wing Wong and Ada Wai-Chee Fu
2010

Keyword Search in Databases
Jeffrey Xu Yu, Lu Qin, and Lijun Chang
2009

Query Processing over Incomplete Databases

Yunjun Gao and Xiaoye Miao

ISBN: 978-3-031-00735-4   paperback
ISBN: 978-3-031-01863-3   ebook
ISBN: 978-3-031-00090-4   hardcover

DOI 10.1007/978-3-031-01863-3

A Publication in the Springer series
SYNTHESIS LECTURES ON DATA MANAGEMENT

Lecture #50
Series Editor: H.V. Jagadish, *University of Michigan*
Founding Editor: M. Tamer Özsu, *University of Waterloo*
Series ISSN
Print 2153-5418   Electronic 2153-5426

Query Processing over Incomplete Databases

Yunjun Gao
Zhejiang University, China

Xiaoye Miao
City University of Hong Kong, China

SYNTHESIS LECTURES ON DATA MANAGEMENT #50

ABSTRACT

Incomplete data is part of life and almost all areas of scientific studies. Users tend to skip certain fields when they fill out online forms; participants choose to ignore sensitive questions on surveys; sensors fail, resulting in the loss of certain readings; publicly viewable satellite map services have missing data in many mobile applications; and in privacy-preserving applications, the data is incomplete deliberately in order to preserve the sensitivity of some attribute values.

Query processing is a fundamental problem in computer science, and is useful in a variety of applications. In this book, we mostly focus on the query processing over incomplete databases, which involves finding a set of qualified objects from a specified incomplete dataset in order to support a wide spectrum of real-life applications. We first elaborate the three general kinds of methods of handling incomplete data, including (i) discarding the data with missing values, (ii) imputation for the missing values, and (iii) just depending on the observed data values. For the third method type, we introduce the semantics of k-nearest neighbor (kNN) search, skyline query, and top-k dominating query on incomplete data, respectively. In terms of the three representative queries over incomplete data, we investigate some advanced techniques to process incomplete data queries, including indexing, pruning as well as crowdsourcing techniques.

KEYWORDS

query processing, incomplete data, missing data, similarity search, k-nearest neighbor search, skyline query, top-k dominating query, crowdsourcing

Contents

Preface xiii

Acknowledgments xv

1 Introduction 1
   1.1 Applications of Incomplete Data Management 1
   1.2 Overview of Incomplete Databases 3
      1.2.1 Indexing Incomplete Databases 4
      1.2.2 Querying Incomplete Databases 7
      1.2.3 Incomplete Database Management Systems 12
   1.3 Challenges of Querying Incomplete Databases 14
   1.4 Organization 15

2 Handling Incomplete Data Methods 17
   2.1 Method Taxonomy 17
   2.2 Overview of Imputation Methods 18
      2.2.1 Statistical Imputation 18
      2.2.2 Machine Learning-Based Imputation 19
      2.2.3 Modern Imputation Methods 21

3 Query Semantics on Incomplete Data 25
   3.1 k-Nearest Neighbor Search on Incomplete Data 25
      3.1.1 Background 25
      3.1.2 Problem Definition 27
   3.2 Skyline Queries on Incomplete Data 28
      3.2.1 Background 28
      3.2.2 Problem Definition 30
   3.3 Top-k Dominating Queries on Incomplete Data 31
      3.3.1 Background 31
      3.3.2 Problem Definition 32

4   Advanced Techniques 35

   4.1   Index Structures 35

       4.1.1   LαB Index for k-Nearest Neighbor Search on Incomplete Data 35

       4.1.2   Histogram Index for k-Nearest Neighbor Search on Incomplete Data   38

       4.1.3   Bitmap Index for Top-k Dominating Queries on Incomplete Data ... 41

   4.2   Pruning Heuristics 46

       4.2.1   Alpha Value Pruning for k-Nearest Neighbor Search on Incomplete Data 46

       4.2.2   Histogram-Based Pruning for k-Nearest Neighbor Search on Incomplete Data 51

       4.2.3   Local Skyband Pruning for Top-k Dominating Queries on Incomplete Data 54

       4.2.4   Upper Bound Score Pruning for Top-k Dominating Queries on Incomplete Data 57

       4.2.5   Bitmap Pruning for Top-k Dominating Queries on Incomplete Data . 59

   4.3   Crowdsourcing Techniques 65

       4.3.1   Crowdsourcing Framework for Skyline Queries on Incomplete Data . 67

       4.3.2   C-Table Construction 69

       4.3.3   Probability Computation 73

       4.3.4   Crowd Task Selection 77

5   Conclusions 83

Bibliography 87

Authors' Biographies 105

Preface

Query processing is a fundamental problem in computer science, and is useful in a variety of applications. However, incomplete data is ubiquitous, due to such reasons as system failure, a dead battery, unstable sensors, privacy protection, and so on. This book covers various aspects of query processing over incomplete databases, which has become an increasingly important yet challenging research topic because of the universality of data incompleteness. Query processing over incomplete databases attempts to find a set of qualified objects from a specified incomplete dataset in order to support a wide spectrum of real-life applications. This book concentrates on three types of representative queries in the context of incomplete data: k-nearest neighbor search on incomplete data, skyline query on incomplete data, and top-k dominating query on incomplete data. Starting from the key challenges and the intrinsic characteristics of these queries, the background and definitions are described, as well as some advanced query processing techniques.

This book is aimed toward readers with an interest in query processing over incomplete databases. It offers researchers and postgraduates a comprehensive overview of the general concepts and techniques for querying incomplete data. It can also be an introductory book for newcomers in related research areas. The specific techniques presented in the book are combined with several applications and many illustrative examples to make the book more readable. It is our hope that the book provides insights to the database community on how to query incomplete data and inspires database researchers to develop more advanced query processing techniques and tools to cope with the issues resulting from incomplete data in the real world.

Yunjun Gao and Xiaoye Miao
July 2018

Acknowledgments

We would like to thank Morgan & Claypool for giving us the opportunity to collect our thoughts together and organize them in this book. We warmly thank H. V. Jagadish for inviting us to write this book and Diane Cerra for managing the entire publication process. Without their valuable comments and gentle reminders, the book may have taken much longer time to complete.

In writing this book, we referred to the scientific research of many scholars and experts. Consequently, we would like to express our heartfelt thanks to them. We thank Professor Gang Chen from Zhejiang University (China), Professor Baihua Zheng from Singapore Management University (Singapore), Professor Qing Li from City University of Hong Kong (China), Professor Wei Wang from University of New South Wales (Australia), Assistant Professor Lu Chen from Aalborg University (Denmark), and Dr. Qing Liu from Hong Kong Baptist University (China) for engaging in countless discussions and providing constructive comments. Meanwhile, we would like to thank Mr. Huiyong Cui (now working at Baidu), Ms. Linlin Zhou (now working at NetEase (Hangzhou) Research Institute), and Ms. Su Guo (now working toward her master's degree at Zhejiang University, China) for their effective algorithmic code implementation.

We would also like to acknowledge the funding agencies. This work is partially supported by the 973 Program of China under Grant No. 2015CB352502, the National Nature Science Foundation of China (NSFC) under Grants No. 61522208 and 61379033, the National Key R&D Program of China under Grant No. 2018YFB1004003, the NSFC-Zhejiang Joint Fund under Grant No. U1609217, and the ZJU-Hikvision Joint Project.

Last but not least, we would like to thank our family members, whose constant encouragement and loving support made it all worthwhile.

Yunjun Gao and Xiaoye Miao
July 2018

CHAPTER 1

Introduction

In this chapter, we first present the motivation for exploring incomplete data management. Then, we overview state-of-the-art work in incomplete databases. Finally, we compare incomplete data management with traditional complete data management, and discuss challenges in query processing over incomplete databases.

1.1 APPLICATIONS OF INCOMPLETE DATA MANAGEMENT

Incomplete data is ubiquitous. It exists in a variety of real-life applications. For example, when filling out a survey, some questions may be intentionally or unintentionally skipped by participants, or when collecting medical tests, patients may fail to appear for testing and cause a lack of information in their records. Another example concerns time series databases. There are a variety of application domains where time series analysis is particularly useful such as signal processing, pattern recognition, weather forecasting, earthquake prediction, and so on. However, the transient interruptions in sensor readings, such as those caused by incorrect hardware design, improper calibration, or by low battery levels, may lead to voids in the time series [Brinis et al., 2014]. In addition, in many mobile applications, publicly viewable satellite map services have missing map data; in privacy-preserving applications, the data is incomplete deliberately in order to preserve the sensitivity of attribute values. In this book, we investigate the datasets containing some incomplete objects with missing attribute values (i.e., some but not all attribute values from an existing object).

Take a typical *MovieLens* dataset from a movie recommender system[1] as an example. *MovieLens* includes a group of movie ratings from audiences, where every movie is represented as a multi-dimensional object, with each dimension corresponding to a rating in the range of $[1, 5]$ from one audience. In general, a higher rating indicates a better recognition. For instance, given two movies $o_1 = (5, 3, 4)$ and $o_2 = (3, 3, 2)$, we understand that there are three audiences scoring o_1 and o_2, in which the first audience (w.r.t. the first dimension) scores o_1 and o_2 as 5 and 3, respectively, the second audience (w.r.t. the second dimension) scores both o_1 and o_2 as 3, and the third audience (w.r.t. the third dimension) scores o_1 and o_2 as 4 and 2, respectively.

In a real movie recommender system, it is very common that the ratings from some users are *missing*, because a user tends to only rate those movies he or she knows. As a result, every movie is denoted as a multi-dimensional object with some *blank* (i.e., *incomplete*) dimensions.

[1]Available at http://www.imdb.com/.

Therefore, the set of movie ratings is incomplete. As shown in Table 1.1, since the audience a_2 watches the last three movies m_2, m_3, and m_4 but not the first one m_1, i.e., *Schindler's List (1993)*, a_2 only rates movies m_2, m_3, and m_4.

Table 1.1: Illustration of an incomplete movie rating dataset

ID	Film Name	Ratings from Audience				
		a_1	a_2	a_3	a_4	a_5
m_1	Schindler's List (1993)	-	-	3	4	2
m_2	The Godfather (1972)	5	3	4	-	-
m_3	The Silence of the Lambs (1991)	-	2	1	5	3
m_4	Star Wars (1977)	3	1	5	3	4

In the following, we give some representative application scenarios of incomplete data, including bio-informatics, economics, medical diagnosis, and environmentology.

Bio-informatics. Information for the modeling and simulation of molecular interaction networks is often incomplete (missing parameter values, lack of details on reaction mechanisms) [de Jong and Ropers, 2006]. On the other hand, high throughput gene expression profiling techniques (e.g., cDNA microarray technology) usually suffer from missing value problems due to various experimental reasons [Liew et al., 2011]. In addition, analyzing biochemical pathways remains far from straightforward owing to the nature of the databases, which are often heterogeneous, incomplete, or inconsistent [Deville et al., 2003]. As a result, compound graph, reaction graph, bipartite graph, and hypergraph are used for modeling the data, concentrating on those concerned with the structural aspects of biochemical networks.

Economics. In most economic applications, complete information is not always available. As an example, matrices containing information on flows-trade (e.g., income and migration flows) are usually not constructed from direct observation but are rather estimated, since the compilation of the information required is often extremely expensive and time consuming. When it comes to economic efficiency measurement, incomplete price information is also derived by considering cost control. Note that economic efficiency computation requires complete and accurate price information. However, it cannot be always satisfied [Fernández-Vázquez, 2010, Kuosmanen and Post, 2001]. Besides, foreign direct investment (FDI) plays an extraordinary role in developing countries, and its fluctuations reflect the change of influencing factors during time, and therefore, the models to simulate and forecast the trends are of great significance. Nonetheless, unreliable sources (including FDI policy, industrial structure adjustment, exchange rates, and economic crisis) are the most intuitive reasons for incomplete data [Wang and Chen, 2011].

Medical diagnosis. It is not uncommon, in medical diagnosis, that patients' symptoms differ from person to person. Physicians typically make subjective decisions based on past experience. Thus, incompleteness of medical data is often caused by insufficient data compilation, in other words, missing records, and heterogeneous sources, that is, the different symptoms for every patients. Studies on medical diagnosis with incomplete data are of great importance for the potential of helping medical doctors in their daily practice and preventing unnecessary treatment [Abreu et al., 2014, Hassanzadeh et al., 2015, Zaffalon et al., 2003].

Environmentology. More and more persons are gradually aware of the importance of environmental quality and realizing it's deteriorating increasingly as a result of rapid economical development. Environmental data analysis has received much attention recently in many scenarios, such as environmental emission estimation, future emission trend prediction, and so forth. Missing data incurs a general problem in environmental research, usually due to insufficient data compilation, device faults, and heterogeneous sources [Miyama and Managi, 2014, Plaia and Bondì, 2006, Schneider, 2001].

With the scenarios mentioned above, although we can simply perform all the analysis tasks based on complete datasets by ignoring all the incomplete data, the output might be biased or inaccurate. As reported by Gartner [Friedman and Smith, 2011], poor data quality is a primary reason for 40% of all business initiatives failing to achieve their targeted benefits, and data quality affects overall labor productivity by as much as 20%. Hence, the problem of handling incomplete data is studied at the beginning of research [Graham, 2012, Imieliński and Lipski Jr, 1984].

1.2 OVERVIEW OF INCOMPLETE DATABASES

In this overview, we first review the traditional index structures for incomplete databases. Then, we survey the existing queries over incomplete databases. Finally, we overview the existing management systems struggling with incomplete data.

In most database applications, one has to deal with incomplete data. This fact has been recognized almost immediately after the birth of the relational model, and yet for a long time the treatment of incomplete information did not receive the attention that it deserved. The study on incomplete data starts from the beginning of research, which has received considerable attention in the database community [Abiteboul et al., 1995]. On the theoretical side, the foundational research from the 1980s, first by Imieliński and Lipski Jr [1984] and then by Abiteboul, Kanellakis, and Grahne [Abiteboul et al., 1991], provide models of incompleteness appropriate for handling queries in different relational languages, and establish the computational costs of the key tasks associated with those models.

An incomplete database simply is a set of complete databases (called *possible worlds*). Since an incomplete database provides different possible statuses of the real world, a query may return a set of answers for each possible world [Greco et al., 2012]. The answers are classified into certainly true, certainly false, or unknown. In recent years, Libkin presented a series of important and deep studies [Libkin, 2011, 2014, 2016a,b] on the theoretical models and complexity of query answering with incomplete information.

It is worth mentioning that incomplete databases are those where the values of some attributes are missing without any knowledge on the absent of missing values. It is different from probabilistic databases [Chen and Lian, 2012, Dan et al., 2011, Van den Broeck and Suciu, 2017], which rely on the representation systems for incomplete information and add the probability space over the possible worlds. In other words, the values of some attributes in probabilistic databases are uncertain and known with some probabilities, e.g., following the tuple-level and attribute-level uncertainty [Ilyas and Soliman, 2011].

1.2.1   INDEXING INCOMPLETE DATABASES

The basic index approach to incomplete datasets is to replace the missing values with an indicator, and then index the resulting dataset using a conventional technique, like the R-tree [Guttman, 1984]. The problem with this approach is that all the objects having missing values on a specified dimension will be projected into the same value of the hyper-region. If the proportion of missing values is large, it incurs a highly skewed data space. In addition, in order to perform a query involving k attributes, it is necessary to search for all the objects that match the query object on their observed values, including objects having missing values.

Consider, for example, a query that involves 3 attributes (1; 2; 3), then all the following objects (1, 2, 3), (−, 2, 3), (1, −, 3), (1, 2, −), (−, −, 3), (−, 2, −), (1, −, −), and (−, −, −) are matching objects for the query where every dashed line denotes a missing value. This is achieved by processing a number of subqueries which contain the query objects with all the combinations of missing and observed values in the attributes. Formally, the number of subqueries is given by 2^k. This strategy is very simple and easy to implement. However, its main drawback is that the search space grows exponentially with the growing dimension of the data, incurring poor query performance [Canahuate et al., 2006]. In particular, when there is only 10% missing data for each attribute, the time cost is 23 times worse than if the dataset is complete, which we know from the experiments conducted on an R-tree index over the different datasets and executed 2-dimensional queries with a global selectivity of 25% [Canahuate et al., 2006].

In order to address the problem of *skew* caused by data projection into a single indicator value, Ooi et al. [1998] define a function that replaces the missing values with distinguished indicator values, and randomly scatters the objects within the dimensions where missing data occurred. Two techniques for indexing databases with missing data are proposed, that is, the bitstring-augmented method and the multiple one-dimensional, one-attribute index called MOSAIC. For the bitstring-augmented index, the average of the non-missing values is used as a mapping function for the missing values. The goal is to avoid skewing the data by assigning missing values to several distinct values. Nevertheless, using this method, it becomes necessary to transform the initial query involving k attributes into 2^k subqueries, making the technique infeasible for large k. As an example, Table 1.2 shows all the subquery search keys for a point query (1; 2; 3) using bitstring-augmented index. It is observed that the subqueries are constructed such that queries looking for tuples with missing values look only in a tight point as implied by the mapping function. For instance, for the tuple $(1, -, 3)$ in Row 6 of Table 1.2, we need only to look for point $(1, 2, 3)$ rather than the entire line defined by $(1, [0, \infty), 3)$.

Table 1.2: A point query $(1; 2; 3)$ using bitstring-augmented index

Matching Tuples	Subquery Search Key
$(-,-,-)$	$(0, 0, 0)$
$(-,-, 3)$	$(3, 3, 3)$
$(-, 2, -)$	$(2, 2, 2)$
$(-, 2, 3)$	$(2.5, 2, 3)$
$(1, -, -)$	$(1, 1, 1)$
$(1, -, 3)$	$(1, 2, 3)$
$(1, 2, -)$	$(1, 2, 1.5)$
$(1, 2, 3)$	$(1, 2, 3)$

MOSAIC is composed of a set of B^+-trees where missing data is mapped to a distinguished value. It transforms the initial query involving k attributes into $2k$ subqueries. What makes MOSAIC better than the bitstring-augmented index for point queries is that it uses independent index for every dimension. Nonetheless, using several B^+-trees, the query has to be decomposed, and intersection and union operations need to be performed to obtain the final result. Queries that could gain a greater performance benefit by utilizing multiple-dimension indexes would not achieve it using this technique. Consequently, MOSAIC is inapplicable to multiple-dimension range queries, or other queries where the number of matches associated with a single dimension is high.

Based on the indicators of missing data, Canahuate et al. [2006] present an extended variation of bitmaps and vector approximation (VA) files capable of operating on incomplete datasets. When bitmaps are employed to index incomplete datasets, each attribute acquires an extra bitmap to denote missing values of the data objects on that attribute. Specifically, for the construction of bitmap index, an object o is represented by a bit string with $\sum_{i=1}^{d}(C_i + 1)$ bits in the bitmap index, where each dimension of o is denoted by a substring with $(C_i + 1)$ bits. Here, C_i is the total number of different observed values (i.e., domain) on the i-th dimension, d is the number of dimensions, and the extra one bit is used to encode the missing value. As an example, suppose $C_i = 5$, then an attribute value is denoted by a 6-bit string. As depicted in Table 1.3, the equality encoded bitmap index is shown. In contrast, Table 1.4 illustrates the range encoded bitmap index.

Alternatively, the VA-file employs bitstrings to encode the attribute values, and an extra string of 0's to denote missing values. For each attribute, it uses b bits to represent 2^b bins that enclose the entire attribute domain. Thus, a VA-file lookup table relates attribute values to the

Table 1.3: Equality encoded bitmap index

Values	B_1	B_2	B_3	B_4	B_5	B_6
5	0	0	0	0	0	1
2	0	0	1	0	0	0
3	0	0	0	1	0	0
Missing	1	0	0	0	0	0
4	0	0	0	0	1	0
5	0	0	0	0	0	1
1	0	1	0	0	0	0
3	0	0	0	1	0	0

Table 1.4: Range encoded bitmap index

Values	B_1	B_2	B_3	B_4	B_5	B_6
5	0	0	0	0	0	1
2	0	0	1	1	1	1
3	0	0	0	1	1	1
Missing	1	1	1	1	1	1
4	0	0	0	0	1	1
5	0	0	0	0	0	1
1	0	1	1	1	1	1
3	0	0	0	1	1	1

appropriate bin number. Query processing is modeled on a basis that enables deciding if a data object with missing values belongs to the query response or not. A simple example of VA-file is shown in Table 1.5. If you perform a query "return all records where value is 4 or 5," the VA-file will return the records in bins 00, 10, and 11 as approximate answers in the case where missing data is a match. The benefit of these techniques is that each dimension is indexed independently and is searched separately without needing to transform the query to an exponential number of subqueries. Nonetheless, bitmaps and VA-files are not appropriate for large and complex datasets and are useful only for a small class of datasets where the domain of the attributes is relatively small. In fact, the size of a bitmap index grows quickly with the growing domain of the attributes, as each possible value of an attribute requires a proper bitmap.

In addition, Brinis et al. [2014] start to explore the impact of missing data on metric spaces. They provide a theoretical basis for research that supports the development of advanced

Table 1.5: Representation of a VA-file

Data Value	VA-file Representation
6	11
1	01
3	10
Missing	00

metric access methods with handling of missing attribute values. Through a set of experiments, it demonstrates that missing data causes severe skew in the metric space with only 2% of missing values, and drastically affect the performance of the metric indexing techniques. Interestingly, data missing not at random are more prone to skew and raise the condition of distance concentration phenomenon, where the distances between pairs of elements in the space become homogeneous.

1.2.2   QUERYING INCOMPLETE DATABASES

Query processing is a fundamental problem in computer science and is useful in a variety of applications. Query processing over incomplete databases attempts to find a set of qualified objects from a specified incomplete dataset in order to support a wide spectrum of real-life applications. This book concentrates on k-nearest neighbor search, skyline query, and top-k dominating queries in the context of incomplete databases.

Similarity search on incomplete data. Cheng et al. [2009b, 2014] study similarity search over incomplete data based on the *probabilistic model*, in which not only data values but even data dimension information may also be missing. For example, given a complete data object o, if its k data elements are missing, the resulting dimension incomplete data object is of the form $o_c = (o_{c_1}, o_{c_2}, \cdots, o_{c_n})$ where $c_i < c_j + 1, n = |o| - k$, and $|o|$ denotes the dimension number of the object o. Given a database containing dimension incomplete data objects o whose underlying complete version is denoted by o_c, a complete query object q, an imputation method indicating the distribution of missing data values, a distance function, a probability threshold c, and a distance threshold r, it retrieves all data objects whose distances from q are less than r with probability greater than c. Users can give a distance threshold r and a probability threshold c to specify their retrieval requirements. Instead of enumerating all possible cases to recover the missed dimensions, Cheng et al. [2009b, 2014] propose an efficient approach to speed up the retrieval process by leveraging the inherent relations between query and dimension incomplete data objects. During the query processing, they estimate the lower/upper bounds of the probability that the query is satisfied by a specified data object and utilize these bounds to filter irrelevant data objects efficiently. Furthermore, a probability triangle inequality is presented to further boost query processing. They also improve the approach in order to support both whole sequence matching and subsequence matching problems on dimension incomplete data.

In addition, Cuzzocrea and Nucita [2009a] focus the attention on the challenging case of dealing with *incomplete spatial databases*, where geometrical information associated with a subset of spatial objects stored in the target spatial database is missing, whereas a topological layer describing topological relations among these objects is available. They propose $\mathcal{I}$-SQE (i.e., spatial query engine for incomplete information), an innovative query engine for answering *range queries on incomplete spatial databases*. It is able to enhance the quality and the expressive power of final answers via using both the geometrical and the topological representation of spatial database objects. Moreover, $\mathcal{I}$-SQE query engine is improved by employing a data compression approach [Cuzzocrea and Nucita, 2009b], which efficiently represents and computes topological relations in spatial database systems.

Skyline query on incomplete data. Khalefa et al. [2008] explore the problem of skyline computation for incomplete datasets and propose three algorithms, namely, *Replacement*, *Bucket*, and *ISkyline*, for skyline computation on incomplete data. The *ISkyline* algorithm reduces the number of comparisons required for skyline computation using *virtual points* and *shadow skylines*, implemented by using the bucket data structure.

A sort-based incomplete data skyline (SIDS) algorithm is presented by Bharuka and Kumar [2013a] to compute the skyline objects over incomplete data. It employs sorting on columns to prune away non-skyline objects early, with the hypothesis that, if a data object has been processed as many times as the number of complete dimensions in it, it is a skyline object. Lee et al. [2016a] propose a new sorting-based bucket skyline algorithm, using two optimization techniques: bucket and point level orders. Zhang et al. [2016a] present a general framework COBO (compared one by one) for skyline computation on incomplete data. Zhang et al. [2017] propose a novel skyline definition utilizing probabilistic model on incomplete data where each point has a probability to be in the skyline. In particular, it returns K points with the highest skyline probabilities. Gulzar et al. [2017] survey and analyze the previous studies proposed to process skyline queries in the incomplete database.

Zhang et al. [2010b] propose a generalized framework to guide the extension of the skyline query from conventional definition to different variants, in which an incomplete dataset is converted to a corresponding complete dataset by plugging in estimated values for the missing dimensional values. Specifically, the approach plugs in the value of missing dimension i using a probability distribution function (pdf) formed by non-missing values on dimension i. A generic mapping is then defined, to convert an incomplete point p to a complete point p', by retaining all non-missing values and estimating the concrete value for each missing values based on the known pdf on that dimension. However, such substitution may only be adaptive when the fraction of missing data is small.

In addition, several interesting and popular variants of skyline queries on incomplete data have also been studied, including k-skyband query, constrained skyline query, group-by skyline query on incomplete data, etc. Given an incomplete dataset S, a k-skyband query over S [Gao et al., 2014, Miao et al., 2013] retrieves the set S_k of the objects from S such that each object $o \in S_k$ is dominated by at most k objects in S. Note that, the k-skyband query on incomplete data could support addressing the top-k dominating query over incomplete data. In fact, the argument k is a parameter of skyline thickness. In particular, the skyline query is a k-skyband query where $k = 0$. An efficient kISB algorithm [Gao et al., 2014, Miao et al., 2013] is developed with the help of bucket structure and the concept of *thickness warehouse.*

In some practical applications, users may prefer to get desirable objects in the whole dataset with several constraints (e.g., spatial region, distance, etc.). For a specified constrained region (CR), a constrained skyline query over incomplete data [Gao et al., 2014] finds a set S_{cs} from a dataset S such that each object in S_{cs} is within CR and not dominated by other objects inside CR. Gao et al. [2014] developed BC algorithm to solve this query, which is confirmed to perform better than ISkyline. In many real applications, for all available objects, users would like to find the most preferable objects in different categories. Further, BG algorithm is presented for the group-by skyline query on incomplete data [Gao et al., 2014], which returns all the objects S_{gs} (from the dataset S) that are not dominated by any other object in their corresponding groups $S_1, S_2, \cdots, S_n$.

However, with the increasing number of dimensions, mutual domination of data becomes weaker. Therefore, the result set may be overwhelmingly large and unordered. As a result, the k-dominant skyline algorithms for incomplete data are proposed by Miao et al. [2016b]. It improves the efficiency of time and space complexity in order to control the result size on incomplete data efficiently. Bharuka and Kumar [2013b] adapt the top-k frequent skyline approach designed for complete datasets to find interesting points from incomplete datasets.

To meet users' preferences for dynamic incomplete databases where data items are inserted or deleted, Babanejad et al. [2014] extend ISkyline algorithm to find skyline points in dynamic incomplete databases with the minimum comparison (i.e., it compares only necessary data items, and discards the rest of the data items). In contrast, Alwan et al. [2017] present an approach for processing skyline queries in incomplete distributed databases. It derives skylines from multiple relations where dominated data items are removed before joining the relations to reduce processing time and network cost.

Querying incomplete data streams. Nowadays, a large number of applications involve data in the form of a sequence of values, such as sensor data, online auctions, web traffic, web usage logs, and telephone call records. Usually, these applications are well-depicted by big data streams that involve a huge amount of data coming in very high rates. Queries are stored and executed periodically and, usually, their number is high. For instance, a fire detection application determines the top-k temperature readings from a large number of sensors located in a forest. As another example, a financial analyst may issue a top-k query to a stock transaction database asking for the top-100 stock prices. Hence, data streams are incomplete as a result of various errors, such as data interference, human mistakes, and limitations of equipment.

The problem of tracking top-k items over multiple data streams in a sliding window is studied by Haghani et al. [2009]. Given a dataset and a score function, a top-k query returns the k objects with the highest (lowest) scores. Let $O = \{p, q, \cdots\}$ be the set of objects we are monitoring. d incoming streams $s_1, s_2, \cdots, s_d$ are considered, each corresponding to one attribute of the objects. Each stream s_i contains the tuple of the form $\langle p.id, p.value(i), p.t_i \rangle$, where $p.id$ uniquely identifies object p, $p.value(i)$ is the value of attribute i of p, and $p.t_i$ is the arrival time of the tuple. Objects do not necessarily appear in all streams and can arrive in different streams at different timestamps. Tuples continuously stream in, and they are considered valid while they belong to a sliding window W. Figure 1.1 depicts an example of the model in the network monitoring scenario. Objects do not arrive in the same order in different streams. The aggregation function is *sum*, and a time-based window is used. At each instant of time, it calculates the scores of valid objects given a monotonically increasing aggregation function: $score(p) = f(p.value(1), \cdots, p.value(d))$. An object is considered valid if it has at least one valid attribute. When calculating $score(p)$, the value of an unseen or expired attribute is considered to be the smallest possible in the case where values are normalized to $[0, 1]$. The score of an object can increase over time as some of its unseen attributes arrive, or it can decrease as some of its attributes expire.

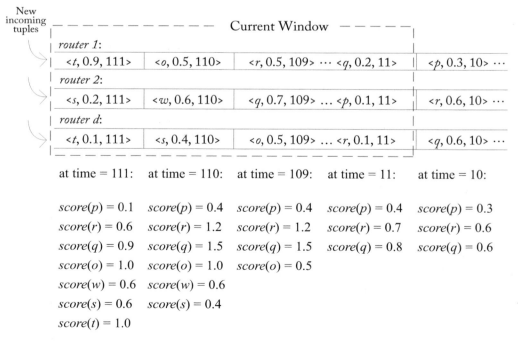

Figure 1.1: Illustration of top-k query on incomplete data streams.

Haghani et al. [2009] propose an exact algorithm, which builds on generating multiple instances of the same object in a way that enables efficient object pruning. They also present an approximate algorithm, which leverages correlation statistics of pairs of streams to evict more objects while maintaining accuracy. In addition, Kolomvatsos et al. [2015] extend the work of top-k queries over incomplete data streams, focusing on the creation and maintenance of top-k lists useful to provide efficient responses to top-k queries, where the principles of optimal stopping theory (OST) is employed. Ma et al. [2013] present a double-index-based k-dominant skyline algorithm for incomplete data streams. The objects with the same missing dimensional values are placed in the same bucket. The different bitmap values correspond to different buckets. For every bucket, they calculate the candidate k-dominant skyline dataset according to two index tables. The two index tables are based on the ability that an object dominates other objects as well as the possibility that the object becomes a k-dominant skyline object. Then, they compute the global skyline objects from the candidate skyline object set. Once an object arrives at a sliding window, k-dominant skyline objects are updated.

Querying incomplete data with crowdsourcing. Some queries cannot be answered by machines only. Processing such queries requires human input for providing information that is missing from the database, performing computationally difficult functions, and matching, ranking, or aggregating results based on fuzzy criteria. As a result, the combination of crowdsourcing technique and querying incomplete data is becoming increasingly popular.

CrowdDB [Franklin et al., 2011] uses human input via crowdsourcing to process queries that neither database systems nor search engines can adequately answer. It utilizes SQL both as a language for posing complex queries and as a way to model data. Although CrowdDB leverages many aspects of traditional database systems, there are also important differences. Conceptually, a major change is that the traditional closed-world assumption for query processing does not hold for human input. From an implementation perspective, human-oriented query operators are needed to solicit, integrate, and cleanse crowdsourced data including CROWDPROBE, CROWDJOIN, and CROWDCOMPARE. Further, performance and cost depend on a number of new factors including worker affinity, training, fatigue, motivation, and location. During query processing, the CrowdDB system automatically posts one or more human intelligence tasks (HITs) using the Amazon Mechanical Turk (AMT) web service API, and collects the answers as they arrive. After receiving the answers, CrowdDB performs simple quality control using quorum votes before it passes the answers to the query execution engine. Finally, the system continuously updates the query result and estimates the quality of the current result based on the new answers. The user may thus stop the query as soon as the quality is sufficient or intervene if a problem is detected.

Consequently, a series of crowdsourced databases are developed, such as Qurk [Marcus et al., 2011b] and Deco [Parameswaran et al., 2012b]. Also, crowd queries have been extensively explored, for example, select [Gao et al., 2013, Parameswaran et al., 2012a, Trushkowsky et al., 2013], join [Marcus et al., 2011a, Wang et al., 2012, 2013, 2015], sort [Marcus et al., 2011a], group-by [Davidson et al., 2013], maximum [Guo et al., 2012, Venetis et al., 2012, Verroios et al., 2015], and top-k query [Ciceri et al., 2016, Davidson et al., 2013, de Alfaro et al., 2016, Lee et al., 2017, Li et al., 2017b, Nieke et al., 2014, Zhang et al., 2016b]. One can refer to the survey work by Li et al. [2016, 2017a] for further understanding crowdsourcing efforts.

To sum up, we summarize the queries over incomplete data mentioned above, including the used algorithms, techniques, advantages, and disadvantages, as shown in Table 1.6.

1.2.3   INCOMPLETE DATABASE MANAGEMENT SYSTEMS

Database management systems (DBMS) play an essential role in the practical applications of almost all fields including education, health care, government, economics, sports, recreation, etc. Next, we survey the existing systems for processing incomplete data, consisting of MayBMS, QUIC, Trio, QPIAD, and SI^2P.

MayBMS [Antova et al., 2007, Huang et al., 2009] is built entirely inside PostgreSQL. It models incomplete data using extended world-set decompositions (WSDs), where worlds or correlations between worlds have probabilities. Moreover, queries in MayMBS are expressed in an SQL-like language with special constructs that deal with incompleteness and probabilities. In order to demonstrate applicability, they also build, on top of MayBMS, a web-based application which offers National Basketball Association (NBA)-related information based on what-if analysis of team dynamics using NBA data.[2] In contrast, the system QUIC [Kambhampati et al., 2007] is developed to handle uncertainty and incompleteness, with the support of decision theory, utility elicitation, statistical learning, and core database techniques. When it comes to the motivation of building this system, in addition to presenting answers that satisfy the user's query, the query processor is expected to provide highly relevant answers even though the exact query intention from users is vague. In particular, QUIC utilizes a decision-theoretic model for ranking answers in the order of their expected relevance to the user. This model combines a relevance function that reflects the relevance a user would associate with answer tuples and a density function that expresses each tuple's distribution of missing data. In addition, a prototype database management system, called Trio, can tackle not only incomplete data, but also uncertain and approximate data values [Widom, 2004].

On the other hand, a system for query processing over *incomplete autonomous* databases, called QPIAD [Wolf et al., 2007, 2009], is proposed, via approximate functional dependencies (AFDs) for attribute correlations, Naive Bayesian classifiers (NBC) for value distributions, and query selectivity estimation from a database sample. Thereafter, an improved version of QPIAD is presented [Raghunathan et al., 2014], which contains mining/learning Bayesian networks from a sample of the database. This method is used to do both imputation (predicting missing values) and query rewriting (retrieving relevant results with incompleteness on the query constrained attributes, when the data sources are autonomous). They compare Bayesian networks with the AFD approach used in QPIAD [Wolf et al., 2007, 2009]. The result shows that

---

[2]Available at http://www.nba.com.

Table 1.6: Comparison of queries on incomplete data

Query	Algorithm/Technique	Advantage/Disadvantage
Skyline [Bharuka and Kumar, 2013a; Khalefa et al., 2008]	ISkyline, SIDS; bucket, virtual point, shadow skyline	SIDS outperforms ISkyline; but ISkyline is time consuming, SIDS does not support data update
k-skyband [Gao et al., 2014; Miao et al., 2013]	kISB; bucket, thickness warehouse	No assumption on index availability and data pre-processing, while the result set may include many non-desirable points
Constrained skyline [Gao et al., 2014]	BC; bucket, bitmap warehouse	BC is superior to ISkyline, but cost grows with the enlarged constrained region
Group-by skyline [Gao et al., 2014]	BG; bucket	BG is superior to ISkyline, while BG does not consider data update
Skyline query over dynamic incomplete data [Babanejad et al., 2014]	InCompDySkyline; bucket, ISkyline	Considers the dynamic incomplete databases, but requires extra memory for temporary structures
Top-k frequent skyline [Bharuka and Kumar, 2013b]	IDFS; skyline frequency metric	Overcomes the drawback of weak pareto dominance relationship, while not scalable for large datasets with high dimension
Crowd skyline [Lofi et al., 2013b]	Model on attribute impact; crowdsourcing, error model	Integrates human work with extra monetary cost
Crowd top-k [Nieke et al., 2014]	TopCrowd; crowdsourcing, probabilistic heuristics	Works effectively on incomplete data, but needs to balance the response time, monetary cost, and the result quality
Similarity search on incomplete dimension data [Cheng et al., 2014]	PSQ-DID; probability triangle inequality, imputation strategy	Independent of imputation strategies, but does not handle other similarity metrics except for the Euclidean distance
$\mathcal{I}$-SQE [Cuzzocrea and Nucita, 2009a]	EvaluateRangeQuery; R-tree, B-tree	Efficient for range queries, while query time increases drastically with the increasing number of spatial objects
Top-k query on incomplete streams [Haghani et al., 2009, Kolomvatsos et al., 2015]	OST; sliding window model	Avoids unnecessary calculations, but relies on observations over a number of streams
k-dominant skyline query on incomplete streams [Ma et al., 2013]	N-skyline; bucket, sliding window	Superior to other similar algorithms in terms of efficiency and performance, but not scalable for high dimensional data

Bayesian networks have a significant edge over AFDs in dealing with missing values on multiple correlated attributes or at high levels of incompleteness in test data.

In addition, a recommender system SI^{2}P [Miao et al., 2016a] recently was developed on top of PostgreSQL, which employs preference queries based on the incomplete rating information for restaurant recommendation. The supported queries of SI^{2}P contain skyline queries and top-k dominating queries on incomplete data, range queries, and basic operators in relational databases, such as selection, projection, join, update, etc. In addition to supporting convenient and flexible query submission and query result presentation, SI^{2}P has functionalities including useful result explanation and dataset interaction.

1.3   CHALLENGES OF QUERYING INCOMPLETE DATABASES

The challenges of querying incomplete data are due to the lack of efficient query algorithms. Most query processing techniques for traditional complete data or uncertain data are not able to support the query processing over incomplete data directly and efficiently.

First, there is a lack of the index structures for incomplete data. For example, it is hard to find the minimum bounding rectangle (MBR) for the incomplete data with several missing attribute values, and thus, the typical R-tree family [Guttman, 1984] cannot be employed for querying incomplete databases. The traditional distance function (e.g., L_2 norm) is not applicable to incomplete data objects (with missing attribute values). Moreover, the transitivity of dominance relationship that serves as the basis of traditional complete databases does not hold for incomplete databases [Khalefa et al., 2008].

Challenge 1.1   How to design effective index structures to support the queries over incomplete data.

A series of queries in the context of incomplete data have been explored, including skyline queries on incomplete data [Khalefa et al., 2008, Lofi et al., 2013a], similarity search on dimension incomplete data [Cheng et al., 2009b, 2014], top-k queries on incomplete data streams [Haghani et al., 2009], etc. In spite of those efforts, the existing algorithms cannot satisfy the urgent demand from emerging applications and users struggling with incomplete data.

Challenge 1.2   How to satisfy the urgent demand on efficient algorithms for novel and complex queries over incomplete data.

Collective intelligence has become a hot topic with the development of Web 3.0 and the emerging of human-powered techniques. Hence, many crowdsourcing platforms [Yuen et al.,

2011] have appeared, such as Amazon Mechanical Turk (AMT),[3] Crowdflower,[4] and Upwork,[5] each of which acts as an intermediary between the requesters and the workers. It is a promising direction to combine crowdsourcing techniques with query processing on incomplete data.

Challenge 1.3   How to answer the queries over incomplete data wisely with the help of crowdsourcing techniques.

1.4   ORGANIZATION

The rest of this book is organized as follows. Chapter 2 summarizes the three general models of handling incomplete data, including the data discarding model, the observed-data dependent model, and the data imputation model. In particular, the data discarding model is feasible only for datasets with *low* missing rate. The query processing under the models of data discarding and data imputation can resort to the query techniques of processing complete data (when the missing values are all discarded or imputed). We describe some conventional imputation methods, for example, statistical methods, machine-learning based approaches, and some modern advance imputation methods.

Then, in Chapter 3, we introduce the semantics of three representative queries, including k-nearest neighbor (kNN for short) search, skyline query, and top-k dominating query over *incomplete* data, respectively. Specifically, kNN search plays an important role in many real-life applications such as pattern recognition and multimedia retrieval, and benefits the development of research fields including data mining and machine learning. On the other hand, either skyline query or top-k dominating query has a large application base in decision making, profile-based services, recommendation systems, etc. Furthermore, top-k dominating query combines the advantages of skyline query and top-k query.

Next, Chapter 4 describes some advanced techniques for processing kNN search, skyline query, and top-k dominating query over incomplete data. To be more specific, we elaborate three kinds of advanced techniques, including index techniques, pruning techniques, and crowdsourcing techniques. For kNN search and top-k dominating queries on incomplete data, we introduce LαB index, histogram approximation index, and (improved) bitmap index. For them, we also present α value pruning, upper bound score pruning, bitmap pruning, etc. For skyline query over incomplete data, we propose a crowdsourcing framework to answer it, taking into account *data correlation*. It consists of two main phases: the modeling phase and the crowdsourcing phase.

Last but not least, in Chapter 5, we conclude the book and point out some open problems/directions for future work.

---

[3]Availabe at https://www.mturk.com/mturk/.
[4]Availabe at https://www.crowdflower.com.
[5]Availabe at https://www.upwork.com.

CHAPTER 2

Handling Incomplete Data Methods

In this chapter, we first introduce the three kinds of methods to deal with missing values: the data discarding model, the observed-data dependent model, and the data imputation model. Then, we describe some conventional imputation methods such as statistical methods, machine-learning based approaches, and some modern advance imputation methods.

2.1 METHOD TAXONOMY

The data discarding model. This method involves removing the objects with missing values and operating only on the complete objects [Brinis et al., 2014]. In this case, the incomplete data is omitted, and hence, does not need any technique to process incomplete data. This method generally applies to situations in which the amount of incomplete data is small and the ensuring analysis is not biased by the data removal [Little and Rubin, 2014, Twala et al., 2005]. In other words, the data discarding model fits worse with cases having a high missing rate. For example, when estimating the average age for some population in a survey, if there are many missing ages, and older people are less likely report their ages, the average age using the data discarding model will be probably underestimated.

    The observed-data dependent model. This model does not discard any object that has missing attribute value(s). It deals with the incomplete data using newly designated models and definitions such as the typical representation system c-table [Imieliński and Lipski Jr, 1984], the new dominance relationship definition on incomplete data [Khalefa et al., 2008], the probability estimation on the distance on incomplete data [Cheng et al., 2014], etc. Instead of converting the original incomplete dataset to a complete one, this model tackles the incomplete data directly. Since the challenges caused by incomplete data vary from case to case, the query processing over incomplete data have attracted much attention from database researchers. It is the focus of this book.

    The data imputation model. This model replaces the missing data with the imputed values. Thus, the incomplete dataset becomes virtually complete. The (imputed) complete data can be processed using the traditional techniques and algorithms (for complete data). Several categories of imputation methods are to be introduced later.

    Figure 2.1 summarizes the three models of handling incompleteness. In terms of the incomplete dataset, the data discarding model and the data imputation model transform it into a complete dataset, and the subsequent analysis is performed on the complete dataset. In contrast, in the observed-data dependent model, the analysis is directly processed on the incomplete dataset (without missing data discarding or imputation).

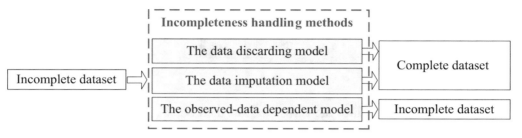

Figure 2.1: Categorization of incompleteness handling methods.

2.2   OVERVIEW OF IMPUTATION METHODS

2.2.1   STATISTICAL IMPUTATION

One kind of imputation methods imputes the missing features using statistical theory [Little and Rubin, 2014]. In this way, the distribution of whole data can be preserved by avoiding bias on data distribution. *Mean/mode imputation* (MMI) replaces the missing data by the mean or mode of all the observed data. In the mean imputation, the mean of the values of an attribute that contains missing data is used to fill in the missing values. In the case of a categorical attribute, the mode, which is the most frequent value, is used instead of the mean. The algorithm imputes missing values for each attribute separately. Mean imputation can be conditional or unconditional, that is, not conditioned on the values of other variables in the record. Conditional mean method imputes a mean value, which depends on the values of the complete attributes for the incomplete record.

In *regression*, the missing components are filled in via the predicted values from a regression analysis using the components of the vector that are present. Consider that the i-th input attribute contains missing values, and the remaining $(d-1)$ attributes are complete. In this procedure, a regression model $f(\cdot)$ is trained to approximate the unknown feature using the available data, that is,

$$\tilde{x}_i = f(x_o) \approx x_i, \tag{2.1}$$

where x_o is the input vector composed of the $(d-1)$ complete attributes. In particular, several regression models can be used to impute missing values, including linear, logistic, polytomous, etc. In general, logistic regression model is applied for binary attributes, polytomous regression for discrete attributes, and linear regression for numerical attributes. Regression imputation is well suited when the missing variables of interest are correlated with the complete sample [García-Laencina et al., 2010]. An advantage of this approach over MMI is that it preserves the variance and covariance of variables with missing data. The disadvantage of the approach is that all the imputed values follow a single regression curve and cannot represent any inherent variation in the data.

In the *hot deck*, for each record that contains missing values, the most similar record is found, and the missing values are imputed from that record. If the most similar record also contains missing information for the same attributes as the original record, it is discarded, and another closest record is found. The procedure is repeated until all the missing values are successfully imputed or the entire database is evaluated. When no similar record with the required values filled in is found, the closest record with the minimum number of missing values is chosen to impute the missing values. Cold-deck imputation is similar to hot-deck approach except that it needs an additional dataset, other than the incomplete data of interest, to conduct imputation.

The three aforementioned approaches provide a simple missing data imputation, which does not reflect the uncertainty about the prediction of the unknown values. They belong to single imputation methods [García-Laencina et al., 2010], where a missing value is imputed by a single value. In contrast, in the case of multiple imputation (MI) methods, several choices for imputing the missing value are computed. Specifically, Rubin [2004] defines MIs as a process where several complete databases are first created by imputing different values to reflect uncertainty about the right values to impute. Second, each of the databases is analyzed by standard procedures specific for handling complete data. At the end, the analyses for each database are combined into the final result. In particular, the *linear discriminant analysis* (LDA) is an MI method, serving as a statistical approach for missing data imputation. LDA is particularly suitable for the data where within-class frequencies are unequal, since it maximizes the ratio of between-class variance to the within-class variance in order to assure the best separations. Moreover, LDA is a commonly used technique for data classification and dimensionality reduction [Manly, 1994].

2.2.2   MACHINE LEARNING-BASED IMPUTATION

Imputation methods based on machine learning are sophisticated procedures that generally consist of creating a predictive model to estimate missing values. The *k-nearest neighbor* (kNN) method is a common method, in which k-nearest neighbors are selected from the complete cases, so that they minimize a similarity measure. The nearest, most similar, neighbors are found by minimizing a distance function (e.g., Euclidean distance). Given an incomplete object o,

$$V = \{v_k\}_{k=1}^{K} \qquad (2.2)$$

represents the set of its k-nearest neighbors (according to a distance metric) arranged in increasing order of their distances. Once the neighbors have been found, a replacement value to substitute the missing attribute value must be estimated. How the replacement value is calculated depends on the type of data; the mode can be used for discrete data, and the mean for continuous data. An improved alternative is to weight the contribution of each of the k-nearest neighbors according to their distances to the incomplete object whose values will be imputed, where it is obvious that greater contribution refers to closer neighbors.

A basic *multi-layer perceptron* (MLP) imputation approach trains an MLP using regression models, in which each incomplete attribute is learned (it is used as output) by means of the remaining complete attributes given as inputs. The MLP imputation scheme can be described as follows.

- Given an incomplete input dataset X, separate the input vectors that do not contain any missing data (observed component, X_o) from the ones that have missing values (missing component, X_m).

- For each possible combination of incomplete attributes in X_m, construct an MLP scheme using X_o. The target variables are the attributes with missing data, and the input variables are the other remaining attributes.

In this approach, there is one MLP model per missing variables combination. Depending on the nature of the attributes to be imputed (continuous or discrete), different error functions (sum of squares error or cross-entropy error) are minimized during the training process. After the optimal MLP architectures are chosen, for each incomplete object in X_m, unknown values are predicted using its corresponding MLP model (according to the attributes to be imputed).

The *self-organizing map* (SOM) was originally developed to imitate the formation of the orientation of specific neural cells in the brain [Van Hulle, 2012]. An SOM describes a mapping from a higher dimensional (dimension d) input data space to a lower dimensional (dimension d_L) map space, with $d_L = 2$ the most extended approach. The basic SOM consists of the nodes placed in a d_L-dimensional array. Each node has a d-dimensional weight vector associated with it. In particular, when an object with missing values is given as input to the map, the missing variables are simply ignored when distances between observation and nodes are computed [Samad and Harp, 2009]. Via the comparison with hot deck and standard multi-layer perceptron (MLP) based imputation, it is concluded that SOM performs better than the other two methods. Furthermore, the SOM-based method requires less learning observations than other models, like MLP [Fessant and Midenet, 2002].

As a single imputation method, *Naive Bayes* analyzes the relationship between every independent variable and the dependent variable to derive a conditional probability for each relationship. When a new example is analyzed, a prediction is made by combining the effects of the independent variables on the dependent variable, in other words, the outcome that is predicted. The Naive Bayes generates a data model that consists of the set of conditional probabilities, and works only with discrete data. In addition, it requires only one pass through the training set to generate a classification model, which makes it very efficient, that is, linear with the number of records [Farhangfar et al., 2007]. In addition, BaysDB [Mansinghka et al., 2015] provides a built-in probabilistic program synthesis system, which builds generative models for multivariate databases via inference over programs given a non-parametric Bayesian prior.

We summarize the aforementioned methods in Table 2.1, where the symbol "✓" is used to denote the corresponding method is applicable to the numerical or categorical values. Here, it is assumed that numerical values consist of continuous or discrete numerical values, both of which could be fully ordered, while categorical values might not have a logical order. Notice that some imputation methods do not work with continuous values. Furthermore, machine learning-based methods are empirically demonstrated to achieve higher accuracy than traditional statistical approaches even though they need much more time. Readers can refer to the comparison studies [Jerez et al., 2010, Schmitt et al., 2015, Twala et al., 2005] for more details.

Table 2.1: Comparisons of statistical and machine learning-based imputation methods

Method	Numerical Value	Categorical Value
MMI [Jerez et al., 2010; Twala et al., 2005]	✓	✓
Hot deck/Cold deck [Jerez et al., 2010; Twala et al., 2005]	✓	✓
Regression [García-Laencina et al., 2010]	✓	✓
LDA [Manly, 1994]	✓(only for discrete)	✓
kNN [Jerez et al., 2010; Twala et al., 2005]	✓	✓
MLP [García-Laencina et al., 2010]	✓	✓
SOM [Fessant and Midenet, 2002; Samad and Harp, 2009; Van Hulle, 2012]	✓	✓
Naive Bayes [Farhangfar et al., 2007]	✓(only for discrete)	✓

In many real scenarios, the datasets often have both continuous and discrete independent attributes, such as equipment maintenance databases, industrial datasets, and gene databases. These heterogeneous datasets are referred to as mixed-attribute datasets, and their independent attributes are called mixed independent attributes. As a result, Zhu et al. [2011] propose a mixture-kernel based iterative estimator to impute mixed-attribute datasets. It is demonstrated to be better than the existing imputation methods in terms of classification accuracy and root mean square error (RMSE) at different missing ratios. Lobato et al. [2015] present a multi-objective genetic algorithm to impute continuous and categorical values simultaneously.

2.2.3   MODERN IMPUTATION METHODS

In addition to the aforementioned traditional imputation methods, there are some modern imputation approaches, such as computational intelligence method, crowdsourcing approach, web source-based method, and so on. Considering the scope of the book, we briefly analyze the advantages and disadvantages of these representative imputation methods as follows. Also, we provide the most relevant references for further exploration.

- **Computational intelligence imputation**. This group of methods imputes the missing values using artificial intelligence methodologies, such as evolutionary algorithm [García et al., 2011], genetic algorithm [Lobato et al., 2015], particle swarm optimization (PSO) [Krishna and Ravi, 2013], and evolving clustering method (ECM) [Gautam and Ravi, 2014]. This group of methods is efficient when the search space is too large and the problem is NP-hard. Nevertheless, it is not a guarantee of reaching global optimal. In particular, two novel hybrid imputation methods involving PSO, ECM, and auto associative extreme learning machine (AAELM) in tandem are proposed in Gautam and Ravi [2015], which also preserve the covariance structure of the data.

- **Crowdsourcing-based method**. This method has proved to be an efficient and scalable approach to overcome problems that are computationally expensive or unsolvable for machines, but rather trivial for humans [Hung et al., 2015]. CrowdDB [Franklin et al., 2011] uses human input via crowdsourcing to process queries that neither database systems nor search engines can adequately answer. There is a host of work addressing the implementation challenges, such as answer quality assessment [Hung et al., 2015, Trushkowsky et al., 2013], matching validation for knowledge bases without enough coverage [Chu et al., 2015], and so on.

- **Web information-based method**. The motivation behind this method is that external data sources on the web are typically rich enough to answer absent fields in a wide range of incomplete datasets, while complete fields in a dataset can be utilized as keywords in imputation queries for absent fields in the same dataset. In particular, the prototype system WebPut [Li et al., 2014] formulates the extraction tasks around the missing attribute values in a database. An inTeractive Retrieving-Inferring data imPutation approach (TRIP) [Li et al., 2015] is proposed to find substitutes or estimations for the missing ones from the complete part of the dataset. Moreover, web (HTML) lists [Elmeleegy et al., 2009, Gupta and Sarawagi, 2009] and web (HTML) tables [Yakout et al., 2012] are also leveraged to harvest missing values. The web-based retrieving approach reaches a high imputation precision and recall, but on the other hand, issues a large number of web search queries, which leads to a large overhead.

- **Rule-based method**. This group of imputation methods is based on rules from logic perspectives, such as editing rules [Fan et al., 2010] and similarity rules [Song and Chen, 2011, Song et al., 2015]. The editing rules are defined in terms of data patterns and updates. Given an input tuple t that matches a pattern, editing rules tell us what attribute of t should be updated and what values from master data should be assigned to them [Fan et al., 2010]. On the other hand, due to data sparsity, the number of neighbors (identified w.r.t. value equality) is rather limited, especially in the presence of data values with variances. Song et al. [2015] extensively enrich similarity neighbors by similarity rules with tolerance to small variations. In addition, Fan [2008] utilizes the dependency theory, which is almost as old as relational databases themselves, to improve the quality of schema. One can specify the semantics of data with dependencies, in a declarative way, and catch inconsistencies and errors that emerge as violations of the dependencies.

- **Hybrid method**. The hybrid methods usually perform better than any single method, via the combination of two or more different imputation methods, for example, combining MMI and kernel regression [Zhang et al., 2011]; integrating support vector regression and genetic algorithm [Aydilek and Arslan, 2013]; combining neural network and genetic algorithm [Nelwamondo et al., 2013]; combining MMI and kNN imputation method [Pan et al., 2015]; and using gray-system-theory and entropy based on clustering [Tian et al., 2014].

- **Other approaches**. There are also some other advanced techniques proposed to fill the missing values, such as using the rough set theory [Grzymala-Busse, 2006, Grzymala-Busse and Wang, 1997], using attribute-based decision graphs [Junior et al., 2016], granular data imputation [Zhong et al., 2016], information decomposition model [Liu et al., 2015], deep learning techniques [Leke et al., 2015], low-dimensional models for missing data imputations on road networks [Asif et al., 2013], a new approach for managing missing data in intensive care unit databases [Cismondi et al., 2013], and so on.

In addition, there is more rich related work on missing data imputation due to its wide applications, including a survey on missing data handling methods within the special context of education research [Cheema, 2014]; a brief introduction [Enders, 2013] to encourage developmental psychologists to begin to use the imputation approaches; a survey on dealing with the tasks of pattern recognition, machine learning, and density estimation from incomplete data [Aste et al., 2015]; the MATLAB toolbox called missing data imputation (MDI) [Folch-Fortuny et al., 2016]; exploring incomplete data using visualization techniques [Templ et al., 2012], and so forth.

CHAPTER 3

Query Semantics on Incomplete Data

Query processing plays an important role in data management and analysis and is useful in a variety of applications. In this chapter, we concentrate on three representative query semantics: k-nearest neighbor search, skyline query, and top-k dominating query in the context of incomplete databases.

There are three different mechanisms for missing data [Little and Rubin, 2002]: *missing completely at random* (MCAR), *missing at random* (MAR), and *not missing at random* (NMAR). In both cases of MCAR and MAR, the failure to observe a certain data point is assumed independent of the unobserved (missing) value. For MCAR data, the missingness must be completely independent of all other variables as well. For MAR data, the missingness may depend on other variables in the model, and through those be correlated with the observed values. This book concerns the missing values that are *at least missing at random*. Furthermore, only the objects with at least one observed dimensional value are considered.

To simplify representation and computation, we use a dash "−" to represent a missing dimensional value for an object o, and a bit vector with d bits, denoted as β_o, to denote whether dimensional values of the object o are missing. For ease of usage, there is also a set-style symbol *Iset(o)* for β_o. For example, the i-th bit of β_o is *on* (i.e., $\beta_o[i] = 1$, and $d_i \in Iset(o)$) if the i-th dimensional value of o is *observed*; otherwise, the i-th bit is *off* (i.e., $\beta_o[i] = 0$ and $d_i \notin Iset(o)$).

3.1 k-NEAREST NEIGHBOR SEARCH ON INCOMPLETE DATA

3.1.1 BACKGROUND

A spatial database is one that is optimized for storing and querying data that represents objects defined in a geometric space. In (complete) spatial databases, k-nearest neighbor (kNN) query has been explored extensively in the literature from last century [Hjaltason and Samet, 1999, Papadopoulos and Manolopoulos, 1997, Roussopoulos et al., 1995]. The query evaluation problem is a fundamental problem in the fields of database, data mining, and information retrieval. It plays an important role in a wide spectrum of real applications such as image recognition and location-based services. The formal definition of the traditional k-nearest neighbor (kNN) query is stated in Definition 3.1.

Definition 3.1 (k-nearest neighbor query). Given a spatial database $\mathbb{D}$ and a query object q, a k-nearest neighbor (kNN) query retrieves data object set $S_k \subset \mathbb{D}$ with size k such that: for any object $p \in (\mathbb{D} - S_k)$ and $o \in S_k$, $\mathrm{dist}(q, p) \geq \mathrm{dist}(q, o)$, where $\mathrm{dist}(\cdot, \cdot)$ is a Euclidean distance function given by Eq. (3.1). Specifically, x and y are two d-dimensional points, and $x.[i]$ denotes the attribute value of x on the i-th dimension.

$$dist(x, y) = \sqrt{\sum_{i=1}^{d} (x.[i] - y.[i])^2}. \tag{3.1}$$

Traditional k-nearest neighbor (kNN) queries have been well studied in the database literature. Most of the algorithms for kNN search follow either depth-first (DF) [Cheung and Fu, 1998, Roussopoulos et al., 1995] or best-first (BF) [Hjaltason and Samet, 1995, 1999] traversal paradigm. In particular, DF algorithm [Cheung and Fu, 1998] traverses the index tree (i.e., the R-tree) in a depth-first fashion. To be more specific, the R-tree family [Guttman, 1984] utilizes the minimum bounding rectangle (MBR) structure to organize the data objects in the tree, which provides a group of efficient indexes for the similarity search on complete data. Although DF algorithm is simple, it is suboptimal in terms of input/output (I/O) cost, in other words, it accesses more nodes than necessary [Papadopoulos and Manolopoulos, 1997]. Hjaltason and Samet [1995] introduce the idea of the best-first traversal and propose an algorithm to rank spatial objects. Then, they develop the BF algorithm [Hjaltason and Samet, 1999], which tries to minimize the number of node accesses (i.e., I/O overhead). As shown in Hjaltason and Samet [1999], BF outperforms DF in terms of the I/O cost and the CPU cost. In addition, there is much effort on the variations of kNN queries, e.g., aggregate NN search [Li et al., 2011, Papadias et al., 2005b], reverse NN retrieval [Korn and Muthukrishnan, 2000, Tao et al., 2007], visible/obstacle NN search [Nutanong et al., 2010, Zhang et al., 2005], to name just a few.

Unfortunately, it is hard to find the MBR for an incomplete data object with several missing attribute values, and hence, the typical R-tree family cannot be used for querying incomplete databases. In addition, some similarity metrics defined based on complete data are not applicable to incomplete data. For instance, the traditional distance function (e.g., L_2 norm in Eq. (3.1) is not applicable to incomplete data objects (with missing attribute values).

Similarity queries on uncertain data are another group of closely related work including [Bernecker et al., 2011, Cheng et al., 2003, 2004, 2008, 2009a, Kriegel et al., 2007, Xie et al., 2013, Zhang et al., 2013]. Specifically, the problem of augmenting probability information to queries over uncertain data is studied in Cheng et al. [2003, 2004, 2009a]. Probabilistic verifiers [Cheng et al., 2008] can generate answer objects' probability bounds without performing expensive integration operations. Another way to compute answer probabilities is based on sampling [Kriegel et al., 2007]. A novel and efficient probabilistic pruning criterion is developed for probabilistic similarity search on uncertain data [Bernecker et al., 2011]. Recently, the Voronoi diagram [Xie et al., 2013] has been used for uncertain spatial data, which are inherent in scientific and business applications. A PV-index [Zhang et al., 2013], which stores the MBRs in a systematic manner, is presented for efficiently answering the probabilistic nearest neighbor query. In addition, the uncertain data index for similarity search is proposed in Tao et al. [2005] and Zhang et al. [2012].

3.1.2   PROBLEM DEFINITION

Almost all the existing *k*NN algorithms focus on traditional complete data and do not consider the incomplete data. As aforementioned, those algorithms and indexes are not applicable any longer for incomplete data. To this end, Definition 3.2 introduces a distance function for incomplete data, which is first defined by Dixon [1979]. This function is widely utilized to support the *k*NN imputation in the classification and clustering on incomplete data [García-Laencina et al., 2009, Van Hulse and Khoshgoftaar, 2014].

Definition 3.2   (Distance function on incomplete data [Dixon, 1979]). Given a set $\mathbb{D}$ of d-dimensional incomplete data objects, the distance between two objects $o,\ p \in S$, denoted as $Dist(o, p)$, is defined as

$$Dist(o, p) = \frac{d}{|Iset(o) \cap Iset(p)|} \sum_{i=1}^{d} \delta_i(o, p)^2. \tag{3.2}$$

Let $Iset(o)$ denote the set of dimension identities on which o has observed values. The function δ is defined as

$$\delta_i(o, p) = \begin{cases} o.[i] - p.[i], & \text{if } i \in Iset(o) \cap Iset(p) \\ 0, & \text{otherwise.} \end{cases}$$

For a special case that $Iset(o) \cap Iset(p) = \varnothing$, the distance $Dist(o, p)$ is defined as ∞. Take incomplete objects $B_1(-, 8, 9, 15)$ and $C_1(-, 9, -, 27)$ as an example. The distance $Dist(B_1, C_1)$ can be calculated as follows. Since $Iset(B_1) = \{d_2, d_3, d_4\}$ and $Iset(C_1) = \{d_2, d_4\}$, we have $Iset(B_1) \cap Iset(C_1) = \{d_2, d_4\}$, and we can derive $Dist(B_1, C_1) = \frac{4}{2} \times [(8 - 9)^2 + (15 - 27)^2] = 290$ according to Definition 3.2.

It is worth noting that the distance function defined above computes the distance between two incomplete objects and normalizes it to compensate for missing values. To be more specific, the distance definition assumes that the distance between objects in the missing value dimension(s) is similar to the average distance between objects based on dimension(s) with observed values. In addition, if there are no missing values, $Dist(o, p)$ is the square of the Euclidean distance (L_2) between objects o and p, and it ranks objects in the same order as the Euclidean distance does. Based on the distance definition for incomplete objects, the incomplete k-nearest neighbor (IkNN) query is formally defined as follows.

Definition 3.3   **(Incomplete k-nearest neighbor search)**. Given a d-dimensional incomplete dataset $\mathbb{D}$ and a query object q, an incomplete k-nearest neighbor (IkNN) query returns a set $S_k \subseteq \mathbb{D}$ of k closest objects to q, that is, $|S_k| = k$, and $\forall o \in S_k, \forall p \in (S - S_k), Dist(p, q) \geq Dist(o, q)$.

For instance, given a dataset $S = \{A_1(3, 4, 10, 2), B_1(-, 8, 9, 15), C_1(-, 9, -, 27)\}$ and a query object $q(25, 78, 36, 10)$, we have $Dist(A_1, q) = 6700$, $Dist(B_1, q) = 7538 + \frac{2}{3}$, and $Dist(C_1, q) = 10100$. Thus, an I1NN ($k = 1$) query returns $\{A_1\}$ and an I2NN ($k = 2$) query returns $\{A_1, B_1\}$. Note that, when there is a tie, random selection serves as the tie-breaker. Moreover, take the Minist[1] dataset as example. Figure 3.1 illustrates the images of digit numbers '5' and '7', and their 8 nearest neighbors according to Definition 3.3.

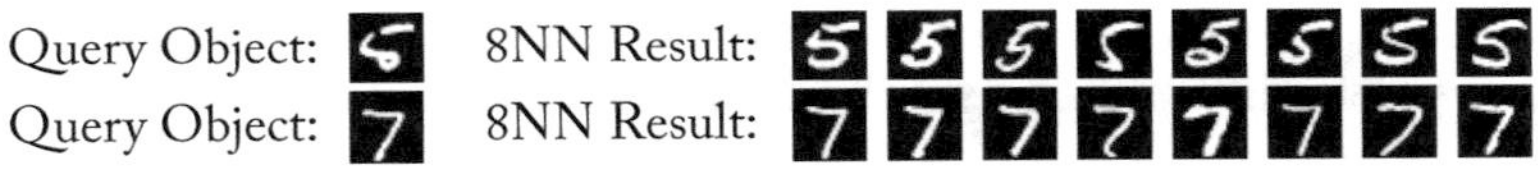

Query Object: 8NN Result:
Query Object: 8NN Result:

Figure 3.1: Example of IkNN search.

Based on Definition 3.3, a naive method to support IkNN search is to rank the objects in non-descending order of their distances to the query point q and then to return the top-k objects with minimum distances for the IkNN query. Clearly, this approach has to blindly explore the whole search space, and hence, it is inefficient, especially when $k \ll |S|$. Is there any strategy that is able to obtain better performance than the naive method? The answer is yes. As to be described in Chapter 4, efficient indexes and pruning techniques are able to help minimize the search space and avoid the evaluation of those objects that are definitely not answer objects, thus improving the search performance.

3.2   SKYLINE QUERIES ON INCOMPLETE DATA

3.2.1   BACKGROUND

The skyline query is a popular paradigm for extracting interesting objects from multi-dimensional databases. Since it was first introduced into the database community by Borzsonyi et al. [2001], the skyline operator has been extensively explored. It plays an important role in many real-life applications such as multiple decision making, personalized services, and location-based services (LBS).

[1]Available at http://yann.lecun.com/exdb/mnist/.

Given a set $\mathbb{D}$ of multi-dimensional data objects, a skyline query returns all the objects that are not dominated by any other object in $\mathbb{D}$. As stated in Definition 3.4, for the traditional (i.e., complete) data, an object o dominates another object o' iff o is not worse than o' in all dimensions and strictly better than o' in at least one dimension, where the dominance relationship has the transitivity.

Without loss of generality, we assume that the smaller the dimensional value, the better. Note that the corresponding solutions are also applicable to the case where the larger values are preferred. The symbol $o.[i]$ represents the i-th dimensional value of an object o.

Definition 3.4   (Dominance relationship). Given two objects o and o', o dominates o', denoted as $o \prec o'$, if the following two conditions hold: (i) for every dimension i, $o.[i]$ is no larger than $o'.[i]$, and (ii) there is at least one dimension j, in which $o.[j]$ is smaller than $o'.[j]$.

Definition 3.5   (Skyline query). Given a dataset $\mathbb{D}$, a skyline query over $\mathbb{D}$ retrieves the set $S_G \subseteq \mathbb{D}$, such that $\forall o \in S_G$, there is no object in $(\mathbb{D} - \{o\})$ dominating o, and $\forall o' \in (\mathbb{D} - S_G)$, there is at least one object in $(\mathbb{D} - \{o'\})$ dominating o'.

The skyline algorithms can be mainly classified into two categories. The first category is non-index-based methods that do not assume any index on the underlying datasetding *block nested loop* (BNL) [Borzsonyi et al., 2001], *divide-and-conquer* (D&C) [Borzsonyi et al., 2001], *sort-filter-skyline* (SFS) [Chomicki et al., 2003], *linear elimination sort for skyline* (LESS) [Godfrey et al., 2005], *sort and limit skyline algorithm* (SaLSa) [Bartolini et al., 2008], and *object-based space partitioning* (OSP) [Zhang et al., 2009]. In particular, SFS is an improved version of BNL, pre-sorting the input according to a monotone scoring function M, which is further improved in Godfrey et al. [2005]. Here, for two objects o and o', the monotone function M guarantees that if $\mathsf{M}(o) \leq \mathsf{M}(o')$, then o' cannot dominate o.

On the other hand, methods of the other category exploit an appropriate index structure, e.g., an R-tree [Beckmann et al., 1990], to accelerate skyline computation. Existing algorithms in this category contain *bitmap* [Tan et al., 2001], *index* [Tan et al., 2001], *nearest neighbor* (NN) [Kossmann et al., 2002], *branch and bound skyline* (BBS) [Papadias et al., 2005a], and *ZSearch* [Lee et al., 2010]. Moreover, BBS minimizes I/O cost. ZSearch utilizes the close connection between a Z-order space filling curve and skyline processing strategies, and designs *ZBtree* to index and store data points based on the Z-order curve. In addition, a generalized framework [Zhang et al., 2010b] is proposed to guide the extension of skyline query from conventional definition to different variants. Sheng and Tao [2012] study external memory algorithms for solving the skyline query and its variants in a worst-case efficient manner.

Furthermore, some other interesting skyline variants are also investigated, e.g., representative skyline retrieval [Lin et al., 2007, Tao et al., 2009, Zhao et al., 2010], probabilistic skyline query [Atallah et al., 2011, Le et al., 2016, Lian and Chen, 2008, Liu et al., 2013, Pei et al.,

2007, Pujari et al., 2015], k-dominant skyline query [Chan et al., 2006, Lee et al., 2010, Zhang et al., 2009], and reverse skyline query [Gao et al., 2015].

3.2.2   PROBLEM DEFINITION

Incomplete data brings new challenges to the skyline query, resulting in the infeasibility of the existing skyline algorithms over complete/uncertain data. One of the most important challenges is the inapplicability of the dominance relationship in Definition 3.4 to incomplete data. As a result, the dominance relationship over *incomplete* data is introduced in Definition 3.6.

Definition 3.6   (**Dominance relationship on incomplete data [Khalefa et al., 2008]**). Given two incomplete objects o and o', o dominates o', denoted as $o \prec o'$, if the following two conditions hold: (i) for every dimension i, either $o.[i]$ is no larger than $o'.[i]$ or at least one of them is missing; and (ii) there is at least one dimension j, in which both $o.[j]$ and $o'.[j]$ are observed and $o.[j]$ is smaller than $o'.[j]$.

The dominance relationship defined in Definition 3.6 is meaningful. Given two objects o and o', if we have no information about their missing value(s), there is no clear judgment on which object is better for the dimensions with missing value(s). Therefore, one can only utilize the common observed dimensional values to decide the dominance relationship of those two objects.

It is worth noting that there are other similar dominance definitions over incomplete data, such as the *missing flexible dominance* (MFD) operator, which is flexible, reasonable, and fair in many real-life applications, as mentioned in Miao et al. [2016d]. MFD distinguishes three cases of the corresponding dimensional values for two incomplete objects o and o': In case (i) both $o.[i]$ and $o'.[i]$ are observed; in case (ii) only one of $o.[i]$ and $o'.[i]$ is observed; and in case (iii) both are missing in order to flexibly emphasize on the existence values. Assume that there is a weight vector $W = \{w_1, w_2, \cdots, w_d\}$ corresponding to the data space D with cardinality $|D| = d$ and a real parameter λ ($0 < \lambda < 1$). Based on Definition 3.6, MFD defines an additional weight for two objects $o \prec o'$, termed as $\Omega(o, o')$, as the accumulated weight on which at least one of the corresponding dimensional values is observed. Formally, $\Omega(o, o') = \sum_{i \in D_1} w_i + \lambda \sum_{j \in D_2} w_j$, in which D_1 contains all the dimensions i such that both $o.[i]$ and $o'.[i]$ are observed, and D_2 contains all the dimensions j such that one and only one of $o.[j]$ and $o'.[j]$ is observed. It is important to note that the dimensions where both objects miss their values are ignored in Ω, and a larger $\Omega(o, o')$ value indicates a higher recognition for the dominance $o \prec o'$.

Consequently, as formally defined in Khalefa et al. [2008], a skyline query over an incomplete dataset $\mathbb{D}$ retrieves the set $S_G \subseteq \mathbb{D}$ of objects that are not dominated by any object in $\mathbb{D}$ based on Definition 3.6.

Take the dataset depicted in Figure 3.2 as an example. Object $f = (4, 2)$ is said to dominate object $c = (5, -)$ as $f.[1](= 4) < c.[1](= 5)$ satisfies. For objects c and $e = (-, 4)$, they both only have one dimensional observed value, and they do not dominate each other, since they are not comparable. It is important to note that the incomplete data loses the transitive property of dominance relationship, which is the basis of almost all existing skyline query techniques on complete data. What is more, as discussed in Khalefa et al. [2008], it leads to the cyclic dominance relationship between data items.

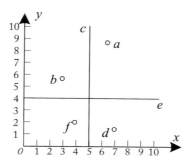

Figure 3.2: Illustration of the skyline query on incomplete data.

In terms of the skyline query struggling with incomplete data, the crowdsourcing technique is able to answer this query [Lee et al., 2016b, Lofi et al., 2013a]. This technique of focused crowdsourcing allows people to take into account several factors, such as monetary cost, latency, and accuracy, to answer crowd skyline queries. However, the work [Lofi et al., 2013b] is based on *unary* questions to impute missing values of objects, resulting in the inaccurate result. In contrast, Lee et al. [2016b] partition the attributes into the observed attributes and the crowd attributes, and assume that all the values in crowd attributes are missing. That is impractical in real-life applications where the attribute values are missing randomly. Moreover, both studies assume that the attributes are independent, and the presented algorithms only support small datasets. Consequently, it is expected that efficient algorithms for crowd skyline queries will be proposed that consider data correlation as well as achieve good accuracy at comparable cost.

3.3   TOP-*k* DOMINATING QUERIES ON INCOMPLETE DATA

3.3.1   BACKGROUND

Given a set S of d-dimensional objects, *top-k dominating query* ranks the objects o in S based on the number of the objects in S dominated by o, and returns the k objects from S that dominate the *maximum* number of objects. Since the top-k dominating query identifies the most significant objects in an intuitive way, it is a powerful decision-making tool to rank objects in many real-life applications.

Take the *MovieLens* dataset shown in Table 1.1 as an example. As analyzed in Section 1.1, each movie is represented as a multi-dimensional object, with each dimension corresponding to a rating in the range of [1, 5] from an audience. If a movie dominates many other movies, it is very likely that the movie is rather popular. Intuitively, a top-k dominating query could identify the k most popular movies for moviegoers.

Papadias et al. [2005a] first introduce the top-k dominating query as a variation of skyline queries, and they present a skyline-based algorithm for processing top-k dominating queries on the traditional complete dataset indexed by an R-tree. To boost efficiency, Yiu and Mamoulis [2007, 2009] propose two approaches based on the aR-tree to tackle the top-k dominating query. More recently, some new variants of top-k dominating queries are studied, including subspace dominating query [Tiakas et al., 2011], continuous top-k dominating query [Kontaki et al., 2012, Santoso and Chiu, 2014], metric-based top-k dominating query [Tiakas et al., 2014], top-k dominating query on massive data [Han et al., 2015], etc.

In addition, the probabilistic top-k dominating query has also been explored [Lian and Chen, 2009, 2013, Zhan et al., 2014, Zhang et al., 2010a]. Specifically, Lian and Chen [2009, 2013] investigate the probabilistic top-k dominating query on uncertain data, which returns the k uncertain objects that are expected to dynamically dominate the largest number of uncertain objects in both the full space and subspace. Zhang et al. [2010a] consider the threshold-based probabilistic top-k dominating query in full spaces. Zhan et al. [2014] adopt the parameterized ranking semantics to formally define top-k dominating query on multi-dimensional uncertain objects.

3.3.2   PROBLEM DEFINITION

Although the top-k dominating query over complete data or uncertain data has been well studied, the top-k dominating query processing on incomplete data still remains a big challenge. For instance, the R-tree/aR-tree in traditional and uncertain databases is not directly applicable to incomplete data. Also, the transitivity of dominance relationship, as the basis of the proposed algorithms, does not hold for incomplete data. As a result, existing techniques [Lian and Chen, 2009, 2013, Papadias et al., 2005a, Yiu and Mamoulis, 2007, 2009, Zhang et al., 2010a] cannot be applied to handle the top-k dominating query over incomplete data efficiently.

To this end, we formalize the score of an object o in Definition 3.7, which is based on the dominance relationship stated in Definition 3.6. Then, with the support of Definition 3.7, we define the top-k dominating query on incomplete data in Definition 3.8.

Definition 3.7   (**Score**). Given an incomplete dataset $\mathbb{D}$ and an object $o \in \mathbb{D}$, the score of o, denoted as $\mathsf{score}(o)$, is the number of the objects $o' \in (\mathbb{D} - \{o\})$ that are dominated by o, i.e., $\mathsf{score}(o) = |\{o' \in (\mathbb{D} - \{o\}) \mid o \prec o'\}|$.

Consider the four movies $\{m_1, m_2, m_3, m_4\}$ listed in Table 1.1 as an example. Movie m_2 dominates movie m_3. This is because, on the two common observed dimensions 2 and 3, $m_2.[2] > m_3.[2]$ and $m_2.[3] > m_3.[3]$. Thus, we can get the score of m_2, i.e., $\mathsf{score}(m_2) =$

$|\{m_i \in S | m_2 \prec m_i\}| = |\{m_1, m_3\}| = 2$. Similarly, we have $\mathsf{score}(m_1) = \mathsf{score}(m_3) = \mathsf{score}(m_4) = 0$.

Definition 3.8   (**Top-k dominating query on incomplete data**). Given an incomplete dataset $\mathbb{D}$, a top-k dominating (TKD) query over $\mathbb{D}$ retrieves the set $S_G \subseteq \mathbb{D}$ of k objects with the highest score values, i.e., $S_G \subseteq \mathbb{D}, |S_G| = k$, and $\forall o \in S_G, \forall o' \in (\mathbb{D} - S_G), \mathsf{score}(o) \geq \mathsf{score}(o')$.

Consider the dataset shown in Figure 3.2; object f dominates 3 objects a, c, and e, and hence, $\mathsf{score}(f) = 3$. Similarly, $\mathsf{score}(b) = \mathsf{score}(c) = \mathsf{score}(e) = 2$, $\mathsf{score}(d) = 1$, and $\mathsf{score}(a) = 0$. If we rank the objects based on descending order of their scores, they are f, b, c, e, d, a. Thus, a T1D ($k = 1$) query on the dataset depicted in Figure 3.2 returns the result set $\{f\}$ due to its maximal score.

It is worth noting that the top-k dominating query on incomplete data shares some similarities with the skyline operator over incomplete data [Khalefa et al., 2008], since they both are based on the same dominance definition. In contrast, the top-k dominating queries on incomplete data have a desirable advantage, in other words, output is *controllable* via a parameter k, and hence, it is invariable to the scale of the incomplete dataset in different dimensions.

The intuitive method for the top-k dominating query on incomplete data is to compute the score of every object o by conducting exhaustive pairwise comparisons among the whole dataset, and to return the k objects with the highest scores. However, this approach is *inefficient* due to the extremely large size of the candidate set and the expensive cost of score computation. In light of this, it is desirable to develop novel indexes/heuristics for the top-k dominating queries on incomplete data, which facilitate score computation and minimize the candidate set for good query performance.

CHAPTER 4

Advanced Techniques

In this chapter, we describe some advanced techniques for processing queries over incomplete data, including novel index structures, effective pruning heuristics, and the promising crowd-sourcing techniques.

Imagine a real scenario of location recommendation systems where users can upload some photos taken in different places in a city and would like to get interesting similar location photos (i.e., querying by images). In general, the photos have various quality levels, thus with some missing pixels due to camera device limitation, light influence, or environmental factors. As a result, k nearest neighbor search on incomplete data can be employed to recommend similar location photos for users. Furthermore, in many cases, users also have extra preferences on some kinds of locations. For instance, they expect to get a group of restaurant locations with higher ratings in restaurant food style, environment, service, etc. However, the ratings are usually incomplete in practical applications [Miao et al., 2016a]. In this case, the skyline query is preferably utilized over the restaurant ratings with missing information to recommend the attractive restaurants. In addition, for achieving controllable output size, the top-k dominating query over incomplete ratings is also a promising alternative.

Therefore, starting from this real recommendation scenario, in this chapter, we introduce some advanced techniques on top of the k-nearest neighbor query, skyline query, and top-k dominating query over incomplete databases.

4.1 INDEX STRUCTURES

The indexing technique is one of the most important tools in the database community to store and search databases. It is one of the main entrances to query processing over the databases. On the one hand, as analyzed in Chapter 3, the traditional index structures for complete data are not applicable to the incomplete data anymore. On the other hand, the query-dependent index is in general more efficient, since it is designated for the specific query.

4.1.1 LαB INDEX FOR k-NEAREST NEIGHBOR SEARCH ON INCOMPLETE DATA

According to Definition 3.3, the incomplete k-nearest neighbor (IkNN) query returns a set $S_k \subseteq \mathbb{D}$ of the k closest objects to the query point q. In order to facilitate the IkNN search, the LαB index is designed, whose name follows the main techniques it utilizes, including the *lattice* and *bucket* structures, and the defined α value of the incomplete object.

LαB is an efficient structure whose main framework is depicted in Figure 4.1. Specifically, LαB organizes and clusters incomplete data objects by a two-layer structure including a lattice layer and a bucket layer. For the coarse (lattice) layer, LαB employs the lattice structure to cluster the buckets based on the total number of observed dimensions (i.e., $|Iset|$). Note that $Iset(o)$ denotes the observed dimension identities for a certain object o. The objects in the same lattice have the identical number of observed dimensional values, e.g., lattice $L[1]$ contains the buckets $B_{11}, B_{12}, \cdots, B_{1n}$ with only one observed dimension as shown in Figure 4.1 (if there are n buckets in $L[1]$). Correspondingly, given a d-dimensional incomplete dataset $\mathbb{D}$, there are at most d lattices.

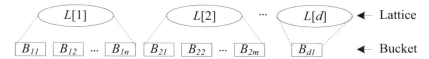

Figure 4.1: Exemplary LαB structure.

In the fine (bucket) layer, for every lattice, LαB partitions objects o in the lattice into buckets based on $Iset(o)$ sets, and the objects in the same buckets share the same $Iset(o)$ set. Each bucket O is stored in the form of $\langle Iset(O), \langle \alpha(o_1), o_1 \rangle, \langle \alpha(o_2), o_2 \rangle, \cdots, \langle \alpha(o_m), o_m \rangle \rangle$ if there are m objects in the bucket O, where o_i ($i = 1, 2, \cdots, m$) represents the data object with $Iset(o_i) = Iset(O)$, and $\alpha(o_i)$ is the α value of o_i (to be introduced later). The objects in every bucket are stored in the non-descending order of their α values, i.e., $\alpha(o_1) \leq (o_2) \leq \cdots \leq \alpha(o_m)$. It is easy to conclude that there are at most d buckets in lattice $L[1]$ (i.e., the number of buckets $n \leq d$ in $L[1]$ of Figure 4.1), and there is at most one bucket in lattice $L[d]$, because there are d possible $Iset$s which have one observed dimension, and there is only one possible $Iset$ that has no missing dimension. In general, the maximum number of buckets in lattice $L[i]$ is C_d^i, where d refers to the total number of dimensions. Consequently, the total number of buckets in all lattices is bounded by $2^d - 1$. Roughly speaking, the bucket structure and the lattice structure are actually hash tables by different keys, in which the cardinality of $Iset$, i.e., $|Iset|$, is the key for the lattice, and the set $Iset$ is the key for the bucket.

Recall that, in LαB, the objects in every bucket are sorted based on their α values. Thus, we introduce the definition of α value of a data object in Definition 4.1, where we can observe that the α value of an object is only dependent on the object, and it provides some clue to the distance from the object to a query object, presented in Heuristic 4.3.

Definition 4.1   (α **value**). Given an object o in a d-dimensional incomplete dataset $\mathbb{D}$ (i.e., $o \in \mathbb{D}$), its α value, denoted as $\alpha(o)$, is defined as

$$\alpha(o) = \frac{\sum_{i \in Iset(o)} o.[i]}{Iset(o)}. \tag{4.1}$$

In fact, the α value $\alpha(o)$ is the average of the observed dimensional values of o. Take objects $A_1(3, 4, 10, 2)$ and $B_1(-, 8, 9, 15)$ as an example. $\alpha(A_1) = \frac{3+4+10+2}{4} \approx 4.8$, and $\alpha(B_1) = \frac{8+9+15}{3} \approx 10.7$.

Take the sample dataset illustrated in Figure 4.2 as an example. LαB partitions the dataset in Figure 4.1 into different lattices, with each lattice corresponding to one $|Iset|$ value. Within every lattice, LαB further divides the objects into different buckets by $Iset$ of the objects. As shown in Figure 4.3, there are in total four lattices and five buckets. In particular, bucket D is fit into lattice $L[1]$ since its corresponding $|Iset(D)|$ (= 1); bucket C is fit into lattice $L[2]$ and its $|Iset(C)|$ = 2; buckets B and E are accommodated by lattice $L[3]$ as they share the same $|Iset|$ values (i.e., $|Iset(B)|$ = $|Iset(E)|$ = 3); and bucket A is fit into lattice $L[4]$ and its $|Iset(A)|$ = 4. For each bucket, the objects are sorted by their α values shown in the left column of every bucket. For instance, it ranks the objects in bucket D as D_3, D_2, D_1, D_5, D_4, in the non-descending order of their values. Note that it is coincidental to have five buckets with four different $|Iset|$ values, and have five objects in every bucket.

A_1 (03, 04, 10, 02) B_1 (- , 08, 09, 15) C_1 (- , 09, - , 27) D_1 (- , - , - , 23)
E_5 (16, 36, 48, -) E_1 (96, 24, 30, -) D_5 (- , - , - , 46) B_2 (- , 26, 53, 17)
C_2 (- , 24, - , 81) B_3 (- , 82, 46, 24) C_4 (- , 82, - , 54) B_4 (- , 02, 91, 54)
E_3 (66, 43, 22, -) A_5 (06, 87, 37, 29) E_4 (26, 58, 69, -) A_4 (96, 45, 29, 33)
B_5 (- , 82, 43, 38) C_3 (- , 17, - , 35) D_4 (- , - , - , 85) D_2 (- , - , - , 11)
D_3 (- , - , - , 09) E_2 (88, 55, 26, -) A_2 (60, 27, 34, 46) A_3 (56, 13, 21, 07)
C_5 (- , 02, - , 39)

Figure 4.2: The sample dataset for IkNN search.

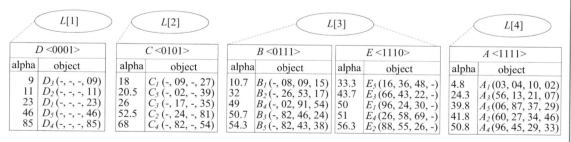

D <0001>		C <0101>		B <0111>		E <1110>		A <1111>	
alpha	object	alpha	object	alpha	object	alpha	object	alpha	object
9	D_3 (-, -, -, 09)	18	C_1 (-, 09, -, 27)	10.7	B_1 (-, 08, 09, 15)	33.3	E_5 (16, 36, 48, -)	4.8	A_1 (03, 04, 10, 02)
11	D_2 (-, -, -, 11)	20.5	C_5 (-, 02, -, 39)	32	B_2 (-, 26, 53, 17)	43.7	E_3 (66, 43, 22, -)	24.3	A_3 (56, 13, 21, 07)
23	D_1 (-, -, -, 23)	26	C_3 (-, 17, -, 35)	49	B_4 (-, 02, 91, 54)	50	E_1 (96, 24, 30, -)	39.8	A_5 (06, 87, 37, 29)
46	D_5 (-, -, -, 46)	52.5	C_2 (-, 24, -, 81)	50.7	B_3 (-, 82, 46, 24)	51	E_4 (26, 58, 69, -)	41.8	A_2 (60, 27, 34, 46)
85	D_4 (-, -, -, 85)	68	C_4 (-, 82, -, 54)	54.3	B_5 (-, 82, 43, 38)	56.3	E_2 (88, 55, 26, -)	50.8	A_4 (96, 45, 29, 33)

Figure 4.3: Example of LαB index.

Deletion/Insertion operation. The update operation for the LαB index can be conducted as follows. (i) Deletion operation: if an object o needs to be deleted, LαB deletes o from the corresponding bucket O that accommodates o. When an bucket O is empty, O is deleted from the corresponding lattice $L[|Iset(o)|]$.

(ii) Insertion operation: if an object o' needs to be inserted into the LαB index, it first finds the corresponding lattice $L[|Iset(o')|]$ using $|Iset(o')|$ value. Then, from lattice $L[|Iset(o')|]$, it gets the corresponding bucket O' using $Iset(o')$ if O' exists. Otherwise, it initializes a new bucket O' for the object o' and inserts bucket O' into $L[|Iset(o')|]$. Next, LαB computes the α value (i.e., $\alpha(o')$) of the object o'. Finally, o' is added to the bucket O' in non-descending order of values.

4.1.2   HISTOGRAM INDEX FOR k-NEAREST NEIGHBOR SEARCH ON INCOMPLETE DATA

In many real-life applications, it is impossible or too expensive for users to get exact query results within a short duration, especially for a huge amount of data. An alternative is to trade the accuracy for efficiency via conducting an approximation search. As an example, in the Mnist database of handwritten digits,[1] the digits have been size-normalized and centered in a fixed-size image with 28×28 pixel values. Consequently, the exact algorithms for IkNN queries on this database may not be able to return the answers immediately, since the query is costly on the high dimensional database. In view of this, we also propose the histogram (HIT) index for processing IkNN query.

The HIT index is structured based on an observation that the closest objects are always near each other in some dimension(s). Specifically, the HIT index separately manages the objects in every dimension. For every dimension i, HIT clusters the objects o with observed $o.[i]$ into different bins based on the order of the observed i-th dimensional values. The dimensional values are disjoint for different bins on each dimension. For a given number ξ_i of bins for the i-th dimension, the observed objects in the i-th dimension are at most partitioned into ξ_i bins. Thus, there are in total no more than $\sum_{i=1}^{d} \xi_i$ bins for the incomplete data in a d-dimensional space. Note that we prefer the bins to be equal sized, and the expected size of objects in each bin is $\frac{N}{\xi_i}$ on the i-th dimension.

For clarity of representation, we use a bin vector $F = (F_1, F_2, \cdots, F_d)$, in which F_i is a bin array indexing the objects o with $o.[i]$ observed, with $F_i.[1]$ as a bin in F_i corresponding to the first bin of the i-th dimension, $F_i.[2]$ as a bin in F_i corresponding to the second bin, and so on. In other words, F_i manages the objects observed in the i-th dimension. To be more specific, for an incomplete dataset with d dimensions, as shown in Figure 4.4, there are d bin arrays F_i in HIT, and n_i bins for each F_i. Every bin, denoted as $F_i.[t]$ ($1 \leq t \leq n$), is stored in the form $\langle key, P, P.size \rangle$, where key contains all the distinct i-th dimensional values of the objects in $F_i.[t]$, and P includes all the objects in $F_i.[t]$ with $P.size$ as the number of those objects.

In order to illustrate the HIT index, we take our sample dataset as an example. There are four bin arrays, that is, $F = (F_1, F_2, F_3, F_4)$, as shown in Figure 4.5. They contain 2, 4, 3, 4 bins on the four dimensions, respectively. For the bin array F_1 w.r.t. the first dimension, there are in total 10 objects with their first dimensional values observed (i.e., $\{A_1, A_2, A_3, A_4, A_5, E_1, E_2, E_3, E_4, E_5\}$). Let the number of bins on the first dimension be 2; then the expected size of objects in each bin is 5 for F_1. If we sort the 10 objects in

---

[1]Available at http://yann.lecun.com/exdb/mnist.

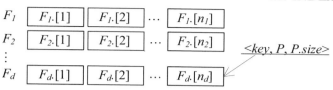

Figure 4.4: Exemplary HIT structure.

non-descending order of their dimensional values, $F_1.[1]$ contains objects $\{A_1, A_5, E_5, E_4, A_3\}$ (with the associated form $F_1.[1] = \langle key, P, P.size\rangle$ shown in Figure 4.5) and $F_1.[2]$ contains $\{A_2, E_3, E_2, A_4, E_1\}$. We will explain later the advantage of packing similar numbers of objects in every bin, and sorting these bins based on ascending order of bin boundaries. Note that in each bin, the order of the objects in "key" and in "P" does not affect the efficiency and accuracy of IkNN algorithm.

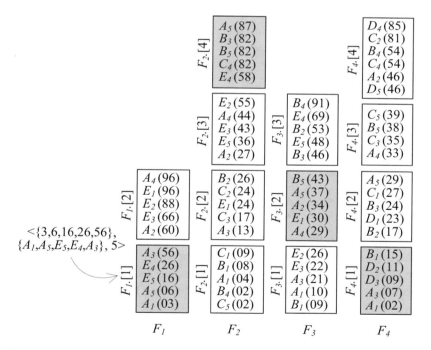

Figure 4.5: Example of HIT structure.

In addition, it is worth mentioning that, in the implementation of HIT index, we use a basic index structure, that is, B$^+$-tree [Comer, 1979], to support the construction of HIT index. Specifically, there are d B$^+$-trees for the construction of HIT index, where every B$^+$-tree indexes the observed objects in every i-th dimension. Then, the bin boundaries in HIT index can be easily derived by the B^+-trees if the number of bins is specified. It is important to note that B^+-tree structure is a typical and useful index structure for indexing one-dimensional values, which is widely used in the literature. A B^+-tree consists of a root, intermediate nodes, and leaves. Only the leaves contain the data objects, and the data objects are also linked by a list in the B^+-tree. The order (or branching factor, denoted as b) of a B^+-tree measures the capacity of nodes (i.e., the number of child nodes) for intermediate nodes in the tree. The actual number of children for a node (referred as m) is constrained for intermediate nodes so that $\lceil \frac{b}{2} \rceil \leq m \leq b$. The root is an exception: It is allowed to have as few as two children.

For example, if the order of a B^+-tree is 3, each intermediate node (except for the root) may have between 2 and 3 children. For ease of understanding, we illustrate a B^+-tree structure to index the objects with observed first-dimensional values, as shown in Figure 4.6. Note that, the leaves of the B^+-tree contain the objects $A_1, A_2, A_3, A_4, A_5, E_1, E_2, E_3, E_4$, and E_5, respectively. In addition, we can easily find that inserting an object requires $O(\log_b N)$ operations in B^+-tree, and thus, building a B^+-tree takes $O(N \log_b N)$ time if N is the dataset cardinality. Consequently, with the support of d B^+-trees indexing the objects in d dimensions, we can construct HIT index in $O(d \cdot N)$ time.

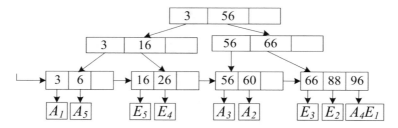

Figure 4.6: Example of B^+-tree index.

Deletion/Insertion operation. For HIT index, the deletion/insertion operation is conducted as follows. (i) Deletion operation: if an object o needs to be deleted, for each observed dimension i of o, HIT removes o from the corresponding bin $F_i.[t]$ if o exists in $F_i.[t]$ of HIT index. Specifically, for each $F_i.[t]$ including o, HIT deletes o from the point set P of $F_i.[t]$. After deleting p from P, if P is empty, the bin $F_i.[t]$ is deleted from the bin array F_i. In addition, it is worthwhile to note that every key in the key set of some bin in HIT index corresponds to at least one object in the point set P of that bin. Thus, if the key $o.[i]$ in bin $F_i.[t]$ only corresponds to the object o in the set P of $F_i.[t]$ (i.e., there is no object in $F_i.[t]$ sharing the identical key $o.[i]$), the key $o.[i]$ needs to be removed from the key set of bin $F_i.[t]$ when object o is deleted from P. Here, the deletion operation completes.

(ii) Insertion operation: if an object o' needs to be added to HIT index, for each observed dimension i of o', HIT finds out the corresponding bin $F_i.[t]$ that o' locates in, and then inserts o' into it, which completes the insertion operation.

Batch deletion/insertion operation. Different from the above deletion/insertion operation, one alternative method is to deal with the objects in batches. In particular, the deletion/insertion operation is triggered by the approaching of a batch of the objects to be deleted/inserted. Specifically, when the objects need to be deleted/inserted from/into HIT index, they are first deleted/inserted from/into d B$^+$-trees, which are used to construct HIT index (as mentioned previously). Once there is a batch of the objects deleted/inserted from/into B$^+$-trees, it is triggered to reconstruct the HIT index by the updated B$^+$-trees.

4.1.3   BITMAP INDEX FOR TOP-k DOMINATING QUERIES ON INCOMPLETE DATA

The straightforward method for supporting the top-k dominating (TKD) query on incomplete data is to conduct exhaustive pairwise comparisons among the whole dataset to get the score of every object o, i.e., the number of the objects dominated by o, and to return the k objects with the highest scores.

It is obvious that the pairwise comparison between objects for achieving the score value is the dominant cost. In the worst case, one has to derive the real scores for many objects (even the whole dataset) via exhaustive pair comparisons, which degrades search performance significantly. Thus, an efficient score computation method is in demand. To this end, we introduce a newly proposed bitmap index on incomplete data to solve the TKD query on incomplete data. The bitmap index employs fast bit-wise operations for more efficient score computation of the TKD query.

As we know, the traditional bitmap index (e.g., Sacharidis et al. [2008], Tan et al. [2001], and Wu et al. [2002, 2010]) is based on *complete* data, and it supports dominance relationship checking via bit-wise operations. Nonetheless, it is inapplicable to our problem, which is based on incomplete data. Hence, a new bitmap index has to be designed to deal with missing data. Moreover, the dominance relationship of TKD query with incomplete data cannot be derived based only on the bit operations. Thus, an efficient algorithm based on the bitmap index supporting missing data is also desired.

Specifically, our new bitmap index is built as follows. First, an object o is represented by a bit string with $\sum_{i=1}^{d}(C_i + 1)$ bits in the bitmap index, where each dimension of o is represented by a substring with $(C_i + 1)$ bits. Here, C_i is the total number of different observed values (i.e., domain) on the i-th dimension, and the extra one bit denotes the missing value. Take the sample dataset (shown in Figure 4.7) as an example. For the first dimension, there are in total four different observed values, that is, $\{2, 3, 4, 5\}$, contributed by 20 objects in the dataset with $C_1 = 4$. Thus, we use a $(4 + 1)$-bit string to represent the values of the 20 objects in the first dimension in the bitmap index. Note that, for a group of values on any dimension, our bitmap index only cares about how many different values are there on this dimension in order to decide the length of the sub-bit string for representing the dimension. Hence, the bitmap index does support floating-point numbers. If every object has distinct i-th dimensional values for a given dataset, C_i could be as large as the dataset cardinality. It is worth noting that the values of C_is do not influence query efficiency but only the bitmap storage cost.

$$
\begin{array}{llll}
\dot{B_3}(\text{-},\text{-},4,9) & C_1(2,\text{-},\text{-},3) & D_2(2,1,\text{-},4) & A_4(\text{-},7,4,5) \\
C_2(2,\text{-},\text{-},1) & C_3(3,\text{-},\text{-},2) & B_2(\text{-},\text{-},3,1) & B_5(\text{-},\text{-},7,4) \\
C_4(3,\text{-},\text{-},3) & C_5(3,\text{-},\text{-},4) & A_2(\text{-},1,2,1) & A_3(\text{-},1,3,4) \\
D_5(5,5,\text{-},4) & A_5(\text{-},4,8,3) & D_1(3,5,\text{-},2) & B_4(\text{-},\text{-},3,7) \\
D_3(2,4,\text{-},1) & A_1(\text{-},3,1,3) & B_1(\text{-},\text{-},1,2) & D_4(4,4,\text{-},5)
\end{array}
$$

Figure 4.7: The sample dataset for TKD query.

Next, we explain how to use a substring with $(C_i + 1)$ bits to index the values observed in the i-th dimension. In short, the $(C_i + 1)$ bits refer to a series of ranked dimensional values in the i-th dimension. Take the five-bit string representing the first dimension (with four observed values 2, 3, 4, and 5) introduced above as an example. The first bit is w.r.t. the missing case, the second bit corresponds to the dimensional value 2, the third bit refers to the dimensional value 3, and so on. We utilize the range encoding method to form the bitmap index. If a value is observed, its corresponding bit, together with all the bits following it, is set to 0. As an example, $C_1.[1] = 2$, and hence, the bit w.r.t. value 2 (i.e., the second bit) and all the subsequent bits are set to 0 (i.e., 10000); and $D_4.[1] = 4$, and thus, the bit w.r.t. value 4 (i.e., the fourth bit) and all the following bits are set to 0 (i.e., 11100). It is important to note that the missing value is always encoded as a substring with all '1's', in order to simplify dominance checking. The bit-strings of all the objects form the bitmap index. We plot the bitmap index for our sample dataset in Figure 4.8, where we also list $o.[i]$ values under v_i columns for ease of reference.

Improvement on the Bitmap Index

We are aware that the bitmap index size (denote as $cost_s$) is rather large, especially when the dimensionality of the search space (i.e., d) is high and/or the domain is high. If C_i denotes the domain cardinality of the i-th dimension for a given dataset $\mathbb{D}$ within d-dimension space, the index size is written in Eq. (4.2).

$$
cost_s = \sum_{i=1}^{d}(C_i + 1) \times |\mathbb{D}|. \tag{4.2}
$$

As a result, the binned bitmap index is introduced to improve the aforementioned (basic) bitmap index. The binned bitmap index efficiently addresses the storage issue by using the bitmap compression technique and the binning strategy. Specifically, the compression techniques are applied on the "vertical" bitsets, such as $[Q^i]$ and $[P^i]$, while the binning strategy compresses the bitmap index on the "horizontal" bitsets, in other words, for the bitstring of every object in the dataset. In the following, we detail these two techniques of the binned bitmap index, respectively.

ID	v1	-	2	3	4	5	v2	-	1	3	4	5	7	v3	-	1	2	3	4	7	8	v4	-	1	2	3	4	5	7	9
A_1	-	1	1	1	1	1	3	1	1	0	0	0	0	1	1	0	0	0	0	0	0	3	1	1	1	0	0	0	0	0
A_2	-	1	1	1	1	1	1	1	0	0	0	0	0	2	1	1	0	0	0	0	0	1	1	0	0	0	0	0	0	0
A_3	-	1	1	1	1	1	1	1	0	0	0	0	0	3	1	1	1	0	0	0	0	4	1	1	1	1	0	0	0	0
A_4	-	1	1	1	1	1	7	1	1	1	1	1	0	4	1	1	1	1	0	0	0	5	1	1	1	1	1	0	0	0
A_5	-	1	1	1	1	1	4	1	1	1	0	0	0	8	1	1	1	1	1	1	0	3	1	1	1	0	0	0	0	0
B_1	-	1	1	1	1	1	-	1	1	1	1	1	1	1	1	0	0	0	0	0	0	2	1	1	0	0	0	0	0	0
B_2	-	1	1	1	1	1	-	1	1	1	1	1	1	3	1	1	1	0	0	0	0	1	1	0	0	0	0	0	0	0
B_3	-	1	1	1	1	1	-	1	1	1	1	1	1	4	1	1	1	1	0	0	0	9	1	1	1	1	1	1	1	0
B_4	-	1	1	1	1	1	-	1	1	1	1	1	1	3	1	1	1	0	0	0	0	7	1	1	1	1	1	1	0	0
B_5	-	1	1	1	1	1	-	1	1	1	1	1	1	7	1	1	1	1	1	0	0	4	1	1	1	1	0	0	0	0
C_1	2	1	0	0	0	0	-	1	1	1	1	1	1	-	1	1	1	1	1	1	1	3	1	1	1	0	0	0	0	0
C_2	2	1	0	0	0	0	-	1	1	1	1	1	1	-	1	1	1	1	1	1	1	1	1	0	0	0	0	0	0	0
C_3	3	1	1	0	0	0	-	1	1	1	1	1	1	-	1	1	1	1	1	1	1	2	1	1	0	0	0	0	0	0
C_4	3	1	1	0	0	0	-	1	1	1	1	1	1	-	1	1	1	1	1	1	1	3	1	1	1	0	0	0	0	0
C_5	3	1	1	0	0	0	-	1	1	1	1	1	1	-	1	1	1	1	1	1	1	4	1	1	1	1	0	0	0	0
D_1	3	1	1	0	0	0	5	1	1	1	1	0	0	-	1	1	1	1	1	1	1	2	1	1	0	0	0	0	0	0
D_2	2	1	0	0	0	0	1	1	0	0	0	0	0	-	1	1	1	1	1	1	1	4	1	1	1	1	0	0	0	0
D_3	2	1	0	0	0	0	4	1	1	1	0	0	0	-	1	1	1	1	1	1	1	1	1	0	0	0	0	0	0	0
D_4	4	1	1	1	0	0	4	1	1	1	0	0	0	-	1	1	1	1	1	1	1	5	1	1	1	1	1	0	0	0
D_5	5	1	1	1	1	0	5	1	1	1	1	0	0	-	1	1	1	1	1	1	1	4	1	1	1	1	0	0	0	0

Figure 4.8: The bitmap index for the dataset in Figure 4.7.

First, we introduce two most efficient and popular *compression techniques—Word Aligned Hybrid* (WAH) [Wu et al., 2002] and *Compressed 'n' Composable Integer Set* (CONCISE) [Colantonio and Di Pietro, 2010]—to compress the bitmap index vertically. In this book, we choose CONCISE instead of WAH. This is because, as shown in Colantonio and Di Pietro [2010], CONCISE has better compression ratio than WAH, and its computational complexity is comparable to that of WAH. Please refer to Colantonio and Di Pietro [2010] and Wu et al. [2002] for the details of WAH and CONCISE. However, we also notice that even after we incorporate CONCISE into the binned bitmap index, the bitmap space could still be *large*. The reason is that the bitmap encoded method we used, i.e., range encoding, is not amenable to compression [Wu et al., 2010].

Therefore, we propose the *binning strategy* to implement the binned bitmap index in order to further cut down the bitmap storage consumption horizontally. Instead of using one bit for one distinct value, it utilizes one bit to encode a range of dimensional values to reduce the index size. Before we formally introduce the concept of the binning strategy, we first present an intuitive example to introduce its main idea. As depicted in Figure 4.8, there are four distinct observed values (i.e., 2, 3, 4, 5) in the first dimension, and the original bitmap index uses a five-bit string to represent the values accordingly. Now assume that we use two value bins to capture the observed values in the same dimension, with one bin covering value 2 and the other covering values 3, 4, and 5. Consequently, we only need a three-bit string to represent the observed values in the first dimension, one bit for missing values and two bits for two value bins. Under this binning strategy, our sample object D_4 with $D_4.[1] = 4$ is represented as 110 instead of 11100 in the aforementioned (basic) bitmap index.

For ease of presentation on the binning strategy, we introduce some notations. For each dimension i, we order objects based on their corresponding values (i.e., $o.[i]$), with min_i and max_i referring to the *minimum* and *maximum* observed values in the i-th dimension. Let N be the cardinality of the dataset, N_{ik} represent the number of objects that have the k-th smallest value in the i-th dimension, and S_i denote the set of objects with the missing values in the i-th dimension. The basic idea of our binning strategy is to employ one bit to encode a range of values. In other words, it partitions the observed values in one dimension into multiple bins with each bin capturing a range. The ranges w.r.t. two different bins are disjoint, and the ranges w.r.t. all the bins in the i-th dimension cover the domain of the values in the i-th dimension. Note that we assume that the number of bins in the i-th dimension, denoted as $(\xi_i + 1)$, is specified, with ξ_i bins for all the observed values and one bin for the missing value.

Next, we explain how to partition the observed values in the i-th dimension into ξ_i bins. We first sort all the observed values in the i-th dimension based on ascending order, and then utilize Eq. (4.3) to determine the capacity of the first bin for the i-th dimension, denoted as b_{i1}. In particular, the first bin of the i-th dimension will cover first b_{i1} distinct values of that dimension, in other words, all the objects with their observed values in the i-th dimension falling with the range of $[min_i, v(b_{i1})]$ are accommodated by the first bin. Note that, $v(b_{i1})$ denotes the b_{i1}-th minimal observed value in the i-th dimension.

$$\sum_{k=1}^{b_{i1}} N_{ik} \approx (N - |S_i|)/\xi_i. \qquad (4.3)$$

Take our sample dataset as an example. For the first dimension ($i = 1$), we suppose $\xi_1 = 2$ and have $|S_1| = 10$ as there are 10 objects with missing observed values in this dimension. Among objects with observed values in the first dimension, there are four objects with the smallest value 2, four objects with the second smallest value 3, one object with the third smallest value 4, and one object with the largest value 5, that is, $N_{11} = 4$, $N_{12} = 4$, $N_{13} = 1$, and $N_{14} = 1$. Based on Eq. (4.3), we have $(N - |S_1|)/\xi_1 = 10/2 = 5$. Consequently, b_{11} is set to 1, and the first bin covers $N_{11} = 4$ objects with the smallest value 2 (i.e., objects C_1, C_2, D_2, and D_3). Note that although $N_{11} = 4$ is smaller than the capacity of the first bin, we cannot increase b_{11} to 2 as $N_{11} + N_{12} = 8 > 5$.

$$\sum_{k=b_{i1}+1}^{b_{i2}} N_{ik} \approx \left(N - |S_i| - \sum_{k=1}^{b_{i1}} N_{ik}\right) / (\xi_i - 1). \qquad (4.4)$$

ID	v_1	-	2	3-5	v_2	-	1-3	4-7	v_3	-	1-2	3	4-8	v_4	-	1-2	3	4-9
A_1	-	1	1	1	3	1	0	0	1	1	0	0	0	3	1	1	0	0
A_2	-	1	1	1	1	1	0	0	2	1	0	0	0	1	1	0	0	0
A_3	-	1	1	1	1	1	0	0	3	1	1	0	0	4	1	1	1	0
A_4	-	1	1	1	7	1	1	0	4	1	1	1	0	5	1	1	1	0
A_5	-	1	1	1	4	1	1	0	8	1	1	1	0	3	1	1	0	0
B_1	-	1	1	1	-	1	1	1	1	1	0	0	0	2	1	0	0	0
B_2	-	1	1	1	-	1	1	1	3	1	1	0	0	1	1	0	0	0
B_3	-	1	1	1	-	1	1	1	4	1	1	1	0	9	1	1	1	0
B_4	-	1	1	1	-	1	1	1	3	1	1	0	0	7	1	1	1	0
B_5	-	1	1	1	-	1	1	1	7	1	1	1	0	4	1	1	1	0
C_1	2	1	0	0	-	1	1	1	-	1	1	1	1	3	1	1	0	0
C_2	2	1	0	0	-	1	1	1	-	1	1	1	1	1	1	0	0	0
C_3	3	1	1	0	-	1	1	1	-	1	1	1	1	2	1	0	0	0
C_4	3	1	1	0	-	1	1	1	-	1	1	1	1	3	1	1	0	0
C_5	3	1	1	0	-	1	1	1	-	1	1	1	1	4	1	1	1	0
D_1	3	1	1	0	5	1	1	0	-	1	1	1	1	2	1	0	0	0
D_2	2	1	0	0	1	1	0	0	-	1	1	1	1	4	1	1	1	0
D_3	2	1	0	0	4	1	1	0	-	1	1	1	1	1	1	0	0	0
D_4	4	1	1	0	4	1	1	0	-	1	1	1	1	5	1	1	1	0
D_5	5	1	1	0	5	1	1	0	-	1	1	1	1	4	1	1	1	0

Figure 4.9: The binned bitmap index for the dataset in Figure 4.7.

Then, we can determine the value of b_{i2} according to Eq. (4.4). Note that, Eq. (4.4) is general, and it can help to approximate b_{ik} values for $1 < k < \xi_i$. Once the b_{ik} values for the first $(\xi_i - 1)$ bins are derived, the $v(b_{ik})$ value for the last bin (i.e., $k = \xi_i$) is set to $\max_i$ in order to cover the remaining objects. Back to our sample dataset, for the first dimension (i.e., $i = 1$), since $\xi_1 = 2$ and $v(b_{11}) = 2$, $v(b_{12})$ is set to $\max_1 (= 5)$, and the second bin will hold all the objects o with $o.[1] \in (2, 5]$. If we set $\xi_1 = \xi_2 = 2$ and $\xi_3 = \xi_4 = 3$, the *binned* bitmap index for our sample dataset is shown in Figure 4.9. Compared with the original bitmap index depicted in Figure 4.8, the binning strategy can reduce the bitmap storage overhead efficiently.

Our binning strategy is *flexible* and *adaptive*. It can better accommodate the situation where there are more objects in one value than in others. In particular, for uniformly distributed data, every bin generated by the strategy contains the same number of dimensional values. When the data distribution is not uniform, our binning strategy automatically adapts to the data distribution and minimizes the fluctuation in query processing.

4.2   PRUNING HEURISTICS

Query processing usually suffers from the large search space, thus resulting in much overhead. The pruning heuristic plays an essential role in the aspect of minimizing search space during query processing.

Although the essential ideas of pruning methods are to shrink the search space for different queries (which is similar to query processing in many other databases), we need to design effective pruning rules/conditions specific to query characteristics, which is non-trivial. In other words, the pruning heuristic is dependent on query type and the specified data structure.

As a result, combining the indexes elaborated in Section 4.1, a variety of pruning heuristics are presented to solve k-nearest neighbor search, skyline query, and top-k dominating query, respectively. Generally speaking, the proposed pruning heuristics rely on either the spatial property of incomplete objects (based on the index structures, corresponding to α value pruning in Section 4.2.1, HIT pruning in Section 4.2.2, as well as the bitmap pruning in Section 4.2.5), or some concepts/queries (relating to α value pruning in Section 4.2.1 and skyband pruning in Section 4.2.3), or the upper/lower bound of scores (e.g., the upper bound score pruning in Section 4.2.4).

4.2.1   ALPHA VALUE PRUNING FOR k-NEAREST NEIGHBOR SEARCH ON INCOMPLETE DATA

For the incomplete k-nearest neighbor (IkNN) query formulated in Definition 3.3, with the support of the designed LαB index detailed in Section 4.1, a novel lattice partition (LP) algorithm is proposed to solve IkNN search.

The LP algorithm utilizes an effective α value pruning. Prior to introducing the α value pruning, we first define a new concept, namely, candidate α range, as stated in Definition 4.2.

Definition 4.2   **(Candidate α range)**. Given a query object q, a d-dimensional incomplete dataset $\mathbb{D}$, and a candidate set $S_k \subseteq \mathbb{D}$ containing k objects, let τ be the maximum distance between a candidate object from S_k and q (i.e., $\forall p \in S_k, Dist(p, q) \leq \tau$, and $\exists p' \in S_k, Dist(p', q) = \tau$). Then, for an object $o \in \mathbb{D}$, parameters α_L and α_U can be derived based on Eq. (4.5) below, and (α_L, α_U) bounds o's candidate α range w.r.t. q and S_k.

$$\alpha_L = \frac{\sum_{i \in Iset(o)} q.[i]}{|Iset(o)|} - \frac{\tau}{d}, \qquad \alpha_L = \frac{\sum_{i \in Iset(o)} q.[i]}{|Iset(o)|} + \frac{\tau}{d}. \qquad (4.5)$$

Take the sample dataset shown in Figure 4.2. Assume that a query object $q(25, 78, 36, 10)$, and currently we have $S_k = \{D_2, D_3\}$ and $\tau = 4$. For a given object $A_1(3, 4, 10, 2)$, we can get $\alpha_L = \frac{25+78+36+10}{4} - \frac{4}{4} \approx 36.3$, and $\alpha_U = \frac{25+78+36+10}{4} + \frac{4}{4} \approx 38.3$. Since $\alpha(A_1)$ (= 4.8) is not within the candidate α range $(\alpha_L, \alpha_U) = (36.3, 38.3)$ defined by corresponding α_L and α_U, object A_1 is definitely not a candidate object, as guaranteed by Heuristic 4.3.

Heuristic 4.3   **(α value pruning).** Given a d-dimensional incomplete dataset $\mathbb{D}$, a query object q, a candidate set $S_k \subseteq \mathbb{D}$ containing k objects, and an object $o \in \mathbb{D}$, let (α_L, α_U) be the candidate α range of o for the IkNN query. Assume that the absolute difference of the distinct dimensional values is no less than 1, i.e., $o.[i] - q.[i] \geq 1$ for $o.[i] \neq q.[i]$. If the α value of object o is not in (α_L, α_U), i.e., $\alpha(o) \leq \alpha_L$ or $\alpha(o) \geq \alpha_U$, the object o can be pruned away safely.

Proof. We prove it by contradiction.

Assume that an object o with $\alpha(o) \notin (\alpha_L, \alpha_U)$ is a real answer object. For the case that $\alpha(o) \leq \alpha_L$, we have $\frac{\sum_{i \in Iset(o)} o.[i]}{|Iset(o)|} \leq \frac{\sum_{i \in Iset(o)} q.[i]}{|Iset(o)|} - \frac{\tau}{d}$, i.e.,

$$d \times \frac{\sum_{i \in Iset(o)}(q.[i] - o.[i])}{|Iset(o)|} \geq \tau.$$

Then, we can conclude that the left part of the above inequality is a lower bound of $Dist(o, q)$, i.e., $d \times \frac{\sum_{i \in Iset(o)}(q.[i] - o.[i])}{|Iset(o)|} \leq d \times \frac{\sum_{i \in Iset(o)}(q.[i] - o.[i])^2}{|Iset(o)|} = Dist(o, q)$, based on the assumption that $|o.[i] - q.[i]| \geq 1$. Thus, we can get $Dist(o, q) \geq \tau$.

On the other hand, if $\alpha(o) \geq \alpha_U$, we have $\frac{\sum_{i \in Iset(o)} o.[i]}{|Iset(o)|} \geq \frac{\sum_{i \in Iset(o)} q.[i]}{|Iset(o)|} + \frac{\tau}{d}$, i.e.,

$$d \times \frac{\sum_{i \in Iset(o)}(o.[i] - q.[i])}{|Iset(o)|} \geq \tau.$$

Similar to the situation of $\alpha(o) \leq \alpha_L$, we can also get that $Dist(o, q) \geq \tau$. For both cases, we can prove that $Dist(o, q) \geq \tau$. Given the fact that S_k contains k objects with their distances to q bounded by τ, hence, the object o cannot be an actual answer object. Thus, our assumption is invalid, and the proof completes. $\square$

It is important to note that the assumption in Heuristic 4.3 that the absolute difference of the distinct dimensional values is no less than 1 always holds for a dataset including integer numbers only. Furthermore, this assumption also holds for a dataset containing some floating-point numbers if the dataset is transferred into the one only containing integer numbers via some existing space partition techniques in the preprocessing procedure. Consider that transferring a dataset into the dataset including integer numbers only is beyond the score of this book; for the sake of simplicity, in our implementation, we get the integer numbers by multiplying 10^6 for the original dataset.

Now we can find the clue that α value provides for the distance to a query object. Heuristic 4.3 explains why we introduce α value and the candidate α range and how to utilize the α value of an object and its corresponding candidate α range to prune away objects for IkNN search. Moreover, if we observe these two values carefully, it is not hard to notice that the α value of an object is only dependent on the object, while the candidate α range is defined based on the object, query object, and candidate α set. In other words, objects with the same *Iset* set actually share the same candidate α range, that is, (α_L, α_U), for a given query object q and a specified candidate set S_k, unless the candidate set S_k is changed. Hence, processing the objects in the unit of buckets could reduce the calculation cost of the candidate α range for IkNN retrieval.

As a complement, in order to cut down the cost of distance computation, the partial distance pruning is derived based on some observed, but not all, dimensions, to disqualify object o from being an answer object for the IkNN query, as stated in Heuristic 4.4. In other words, we can reduce the distance computation cost by strategically performing the calculation dimension by dimension using Heuristic 4.4.

Heuristic 4.4   (Partial distance pruning). Given a d-dimensional incomplete dataset $\mathbb{D}$, an object $o \in \mathbb{D}$, a query object q, and a candidate set $S_k \subseteq \mathbb{D}$ containing k objects, if there is an integer $t \leq d$ satisfying the inequality (4.6) below, the object o can be pruned away safely.

$$\frac{d}{|Iset(o)|} \sum_{i=1}^{t} \delta_i(o, q)^2 \geq \tau. \tag{4.6}$$

Proof. The proof is straightforward, and thus, it is omitted to save space.   □

With the support of the LαB index, α value pruning, and partial distance pruning, we propose the lattice partition (LP) algorithm for IkNN retrieval over incomplete data. The pseudo-code of LP algorithm is depicted in Algorithm 4.1. First of all, LP initializes the global result S_k as empty (line 1). Then, it starts evaluating the objects with the help of the LαB index (lines 2–14). Whenever a bucket B is evaluated, LP first derives the value q_α used for the computation of the candidate range (α_L, α_U) and gets the position of q (denoted as *pos*) in the objects of bucket B via BinarySearch function, whose implementation is simple and hence omitted here (lines 3–7). Note that (α_L, α_U) range remains the same for the objects in the same bucket unless the candidate set S_k is updated. Thereafter, the objects in the current bucket B are evaluated from *pos* to both sides by calling Search function (lines 8–13).

Specifically, as shown in Algorithm 4.2, in Search function, we visit the objects in B from the *pos* to both sides until the condition of Heuristic 4.3 holds or all the objects of B are evaluated. For the object o in $B[pos]$, it is inserted into a candidate set S_k if S_k is not full, and α_L and α_U are updated if $|S_k| = k$ (lines 3–9). Otherwise, we compare o's α value $\alpha(o)$ with the candidate α range (α_L, α_U). Only when $\alpha(o) \in (\alpha_L, \alpha_U)$, the object o may contribute to the candidate set, and thus needs to be evaluated. Notice that instead of calculating the distance from o to q directly, we strategically perform the calculation dimension by dimension using the partial distance pruning, as stated in Heuristic 4.4. If object o cannot be discarded by Heuristic 4.4 (i.e., $Dist(o, q) \neq -1$), the object o is added to the candidate set S_k to replace the top

---

Algorithm 4.1 Lattice Partition Algorithm (LP)

Input: an incomplete dataset $\mathbb{D}$, a query object q, a parameter k, a LαB index L
Output: the result set S_k of an IkNN query on $\mathbb{D}$

1: initialize a max-heap $S_k \longleftarrow \varnothing$
2: **for all** bucket $B \in L$ **do**
3:    $q_\alpha \longleftarrow \frac{\sum_{i \in Iset(B)} q.[i]}{|Iset(B)|}$
4:    **if** $|S_k| = k$ **then**
5:       $\alpha_U \longleftarrow q_\alpha + \frac{Dist(S_k.top,q)}{d}$, $\alpha_L \longleftarrow q_\alpha - \frac{Dist(S_k.top,q)}{d}$ // update α_U and α_L by Eq. (4.5)
6:    **end if**
7:    $pos \longleftarrow$ BinarySearch(B, q_α) // find the position of q in bucket B
8:    **if** $pos \geq 0$ **then**
9:       Search$(S_k, k, B, pos, q_\alpha, 0)$ // visit objects from $B[pos]$ to $B[0]$
10:    **end if**
11:    **if** $pos + 1 < B.size$ **then**
12:       Search$(S_k, k, B, pos + 1, q_\alpha, 1)$ // visit objects from $B[pos + 1]$ to $B[B.size - 1]$
13:    **end if**
14: **end for**
15: **return** S_k

---

object of the current S_k with the maximum distance to q, and the candidate α range (α_L, α_U) is updated accordingly (lines 10–17). If $\alpha(o) \leq \alpha_L$ or $\alpha(o) \geq \alpha_U$, it means that the object o and the remaining unvisited objects can be pruned according to Heuristic 4.3. Hence, the while-loop of Search function terminates. This is because the objects in a bucket are ranked in the order of their α values. Below, we employ an example to illustrate LP algorithm.

Example 4.5 To illustrate how LP algorithm works, we assume that an I2NN ($k = 2$) query is issued at a query object q (25, 78, 36, 10) on our sample dataset shown in Figure 4.2. The LαB index is given in Figure 4.3. Assume that LP first visits bucket D from lattice $L[1]$. To be more specific, it computes $q_\alpha = \frac{\sum_{i \in Iset(D)} q.[i]}{|Iset(D)|} = 10$, and gets the position $pos = 0$ of q, in bucket D. In the sequel, LP visits object D_3 from the bucket D. As S_k is empty, it gets $Dist(D_3, q)(= 4)$ and inserts D_3 into S_k. Since there is no object having smaller α value than $\alpha(D_3)$, LP visits the object from the position $pos+1$ for the objects in D. Thus, the object D_2 is accessed. It calculates $Dist(D_2, q) = 4$, and adds D_2 to S_k. At this moment, $S_k = \{D_2, D_3\}$, and LP sets $\alpha_L = 9$ and $\alpha_U = 11$ based on Eq. (4.5), as depicted in the third row (step 2) of Figure 4.10.
    In the following, LP evaluates the next object D_1. As $\alpha(D_1) = 23$ ($> \alpha_U$), the algorithm terminates the evaluation of the remaining objects in the bucket D based on Heuristic 4.3. Similarly, LP accesses the buckets from other lattices randomly (e.g., $L[2]$, $L[3]$, $L[4]$ in order) in the same fashion. After evaluating all the buckets, LP stops and obtains the final query result

---

Algorithm 4.2 Search Function

Input: a result set S_k, a parameter k, a bucket B, a position pos, a value q_α, a label tag

Output: the result set S_k

1: $i \longleftarrow pos, flag \longleftarrow true$
2: **while** $(i \geq 0 \wedge tag = 0)$ or $(i < B.size \wedge tag = 1)$ **do**
3:    get the object o in $B[i]$
4:    **if** $|S_k| < k$ **then**
5:       $Dist(o, q) \longleftarrow$ Get-Dist(o, q)
6:       $S_k \longleftarrow S_k + \{o\}$
7:       **if** $|S_k| = k$ **then**
8:          $\alpha_U \longleftarrow q_\alpha + \frac{Dist(S_k.top, q)}{d}, \alpha_L \longleftarrow q_\alpha - \frac{Dist(S_k.top, q)}{d}$ // update α_U and α_L by Eq. (4.5)
9:       **end if**
10:    **else**
11:       **if** $(\alpha(o) > \alpha_L \wedge tag = 0)$ or $(\alpha(o) < \alpha_U \wedge tag = 1)$ **then**
12:          $Dist(o, q) \longleftarrow$ Get-Dist(o, q) by partial distance pruning // Heuristic 4.4
13:          **if** $Dist(o, q) \neq -1$ **then**
14:             $S_k \longleftarrow S_k - \{S_k.top\} + \{o\}$
15:             $\alpha_U \longleftarrow q_\alpha + \frac{Dist(S_k.top, q)}{d}, \alpha_L \longleftarrow q_\alpha - \frac{Dist(S_k.top, q)}{d}$ // update α_U and α_L by Eq. (4.5)
16:          **end if**
17:       **end if**
18:    **else**
19:       $flag \longleftarrow false,$ **break** // Heuristic 4.3
20:    **end if**
21:    **if** $tag = 0$ **then**
22:       $i \longleftarrow i - 1$
23:    **end if**
24:    **if** $tag = 1$ **then**
25:       $i \longleftarrow i + 1$
26:    **end if**
27: **end while**
28: **return** S_k

---

set $S_k = \{D_2, D_3\}$. Figure 4.10 shows the procedure of the query processing, in which the symbol "$\sim$" represents the corresponding value not calculated during search, and "$\uparrow$" denotes that there is no change of the corresponding value.

step	object ID	bucket ID	alpha	alpha_L	alpha_U	Dist	S_k
1	D_3	D	11	$\sim$	$\sim$	4	$\{D_3\}$
2	D_2	D	9	9	11	4	$\{D_2, D_3\}$
3	D_1	D	23	$\uparrow$	$\uparrow$	$\sim$	$\{D_2, D_3\}$
4	C_3	C	26	43	45	$\sim$	$\{D_2, D_3\}$
5	C_2	C	52.5	$\uparrow$	$\uparrow$	$\sim$	$\{D_2, D_3\}$
6	B_2	B	32	40.3	42.3	$\sim$	$\{D_2, D_3\}$
7	B_4	B	49	$\uparrow$	$\uparrow$	$\sim$	$\{D_2, D_3\}$
8	E_3	E	43.7	45.3	47.3	$\sim$	$\{D_2, D_3\}$
9	E_1	E	50	$\uparrow$	$\uparrow$	$\sim$	$\{D_2, D_3\}$
10	A_3	A	24.3	36.3	38.3	$\sim$	$\{D_2, D_3\}$
11	A_5	A	39.8	$\uparrow$	$\uparrow$	$\sim$	$\{D_2, D_3\}$

Figure 4.10: Illustration of the procedure of LP algorithm.

4.2.2 HISTOGRAM-BASED PRUNING FOR k-NEAREST NEIGHBOR SEARCH ON INCOMPLETE DATA

In order to solve the IkNN search efficiently, we find the k-nearest neighbors based on the histogram based pruning, with the support of the HIT index.

The general idea of the histogram-based pruning is as follows. Suppose there is a dataset $\{a, b, c, d, e, f, g, h\}$ of two-dimensional objects plotted in Figure 4.11, in which the object c is incomplete, and its value on x-axis is missing. Assume that we have partitioned the dataset into three bins $F_1.[1]$, $F_1.[2]$, and $F_1.[3]$ along the first dimension (i.e., x-axis) and two bins $F_2.[1]$ and $F_2.[2]$ along the second dimension (i.e., y-axis). When a query object q is specified, it can be located in one and only one bin on every dimension. Let position vector $pos(q) = (p_1, p_2, \cdots, p_d)$ record the specific bin $F_i.[p_i]$ on each i-th dimension that q is located in to facilitate query processing.

For the query object q shown in Figure 4.11, the corresponding $pos(q) = (1, 2)$. In other words, $p_1 = 1$ as q is located in the first bin on the first dimension, and $p_2 = 2$ since q is located in the second bin on the second dimension. Then, in order to find answer objects for the IkNN query issued at q, it only needs to consider the objects within the same bins as q. In other words, the objects in $F_1.[1] \bigcup F_2.[2]$ (i.e., objects a, b, d, and e) form the candidate set while the objects in $(S - F_1.[1] \bigcup F_2.[2])$ (i.e., objects c, f, g, and h) can be discarded shortly. The intuition behind the histogram-based pruning is that, every answer object shall be close to the query object in at least one dimension. This is the main motivation to divide the objects on each dimension according to their dimensional values.

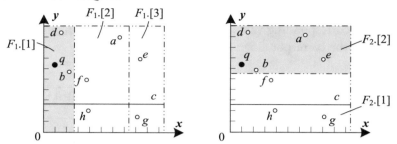

Figure 4.11: Illustration of histogram based pruning for IkNN retrieval.

In the above example, the I3NN query returns $\{b, d, a\}$ as the final query result, which is obtained based on the candidate set $F_1.[1] \cup F_2.[2]$ (i.e., $\{a, b, d, e\}$). However, we can directly find that the real I3NN query result should be $\{b, f, d\}$. In other words, this I3NN query using histogram-based pruning has a false negative, i.e., object f (meaning that there is also a false positive, i.e., object a), where the object f (i.e., the real second nearest neighbor of the query point) is pruned by histogram-based pruning.

We call the IkNN search based on histogram pruning as HA algorithm. We can find that HA algorithm may have some false negatives (positives) when the query object locates near the bin boundaries. In the following, we analyze the false negative ratio of HA algorithm, as stated in Lemma 4.6.

It is worth pointing out that the false positive ratio (denoted as P_{FP}) refers to the probability that the unqualified object is returned by the IkNN query, formally, $P_{FP} = \frac{|FP|}{|FP|+|TP|}$ and the false negative ratio (denoted as P_{FN}) denotes the probability that the real answer object is missing, formally, $P_{FN} = \frac{|FN|}{|FN|+|TP|}$. Here, $|FP|$, $|FN|$, and $|TP|$ represent the number of false positives, the number of false negatives, and the number of true positives in the IkNN query, respectively.[2] To simplify discussion, we assume that there are the same number of bins in every dimension, denoted as ξ.

Lemma 4.6   (False negative for IkNN search). *Given a d-dimensional incomplete dataset $\mathbb{D}$ indexed by HIT index and the IkNN query issued at a query object q, assume that different dimensions of the objects are independent, and N is the cardinality of the dataset. If P_{FN} denotes the false negative ratio, in other words, the probability that a real answer object for IkNN retrieval issued at q is not inside the set of objects in $\bigcup_{i \in [1,d]} F_i.[pos(q).[i]]$, we can derive the upper bound of P_{FN}, denoted as $\overline{P}_{FN}$, by Eq. (4.7) below.*

$$P_{FN} \leq \overline{P}_{FN} = \left(\frac{\xi - 1}{\xi} \right)^d.$$

(4.7)

[2]https://en.wikipedia.org/wiki/Precision_and_recall

Proof. Based on the definition of false negative rate, false negative rate P_{FN} is equal to the probability that an actual answer object o is not located in any bin q locates, i.e., P_{FN} = $\Pr(\cap_{i \in [1,d]} pos(o).[i] \neq pos(q).[i] \mid o$ is an actual answer$)$. Then we can conclude that the probability $\Pr(\cap_{i \in [1,d]} pos(o).[i] \neq pos(q).[i] \mid o$ is a real answer$)$ is equal to or smaller than $\Pr(\cap_{i \in [1,d]} pos(o).[i] \neq pos(q).[i])$. Next, we prove that $\Pr(\cap_{i \in [1,d]} pos(o).[i] \neq pos(q).[i])$ = $(\frac{\xi-1}{\xi})^d$ as follows. First, on a single dimension, there are ξ bins, and $\Pr(pos(o).[1] \neq pos(q).[1])$ = $\frac{\xi-1}{\xi}$. In general, for d dimensions, it is obvious that $\Pr(\cap_{i \in [1,d]} pos(o).[i] \neq pos(q).[i]) = (\frac{\xi-1}{\xi})^d$, if different dimensions are independent. Consequently, the upper bound of P_{FN}, i.e., $\overline{P}_{FN}$, is equal to $(\frac{\xi-1}{\xi})^d$, which completes the proof. $\qquad\square$

Algorithm 4.3 Histogram Approximate Algorithm (HA)

Input: an incomplete dataset $\mathbb{D}$, a query object q, a parameter k, a HIT index F
Output: the result set S_k of an IkNN query on $\mathbb{D}$

1: initialize a max-heap $S_k \longleftarrow \varnothing$
2: **for all** dimension $i \in [1, d]$ **do**
3:      $pos \longleftarrow$ Get-Position(q, F_i)
4:      **for all** unvisited object $o \in F_i.[pos]$ **do**
5:          mark o as visited
6:          $Dist(o, a) \longleftarrow$ Get-Dist(o, q)
7:          **if** $|S_k| < k$ **then**
8:             $S_k \longleftarrow S_k + \{o\}$
9:          **else**
10:             **if** $Dist(o, q) < Dist(S_k.top, q)$ **then**
11:                 $S_k \longleftarrow S_k - \{S_k.top\} + \{o\}$
12:             **end if**
13:          **end if**
14:      **end for**
15: **end for**
16: **return** S_k

Algorithm 4.3 presents the pseudo-code of HA algorithm for the IkNN query. First of all, it initializes the result set S_k as empty (line 1). Then, for each dimension, HA gets the position of a query object q (denoted as pos) by invoking Get-Position function (lines 2–3). The main objective is to form a subset $\bigcup_{i=1}^{d} F_i.[pos]$ that contains all the objects we need to evaluate. Therefore, HA evaluates the objects in each $F_i.[pos]$ that have not been visited, and updates the result set S_k if necessary (lines 4–14). Finally, HA returns S_k, and terminates (line 16).

Example 4.7   Assume that an I2NN (k = 2) query is issued at a query object $q(25, 78, 36, 10)$ based on the sample dataset. The HIT index is illustrated in Figure 4.5. First, HA locates

q into bins along all four dimensions with $pos(q)$ = (1, 4, 2, 1). Then, the objects in the four bins $F_1.[1]$, $F_2.[4]$, $F_3.[2]$, $F_4.[1]$ (shown as the shaded area in Figure 4.5) form the candidate set $\{A_1, A_2, A_3, A_4, A_5, B_1, B_3, B_5, C_4, D_2, D_3, E_1, E_4, E_5\}$. Note that all the objects not in the candidate set (i.e., $B_2, B_4, C_1, C_2, C_3, C_5, D_1, D_4, D_5, E_2, E_3$) are pruned away safely. Thereafter, HA evaluates candidate objects one by one. For example, it first visits A_1, gets $Dist(A_1, q)$ = 6700, and then inserts A_1 into S_k. Similarly, it evaluates other candidate objects as well. Finally, HA obtains the final query result set $\{D_2, D_3\}$.

As stated in Theorem 4.8, we derive the lower bound of the precision of HA algorithm for IkNN search. Note that precision is the fraction of the retrieved objects that are actual answer objects: $\frac{|TP|}{|FP|+|TP|}$. Hence, precision is actually equal to 1 minus the false positive rate, in other words, $Precision = \frac{|TP|}{|FP|+|TP|} = 1 - \frac{|FP|}{|FP|+|TP|} = 1 - P_{FP}$. On the other hand, since the number of IkNN query result is constant (i.e., k), the number of false positives is equal to the number of false negatives: $|FP| = |FN|$. Thus, we have $P_{FP} = P_{FN}$, according to the definitions of $P_{FP} = \frac{|FP|}{|FP|+|TP|}$ and $P_{FN} = \frac{|FN|}{|FN|+|TP|}$. Hence we can conclude that $Precision = 1 - P_{FN}$, and thereby its lower bound is derived in Theorem 4.8 below.

Theorem 4.8   **(Precision for IkNN search)**. *Let N be the cardinality of the dataset, d be the number of dimensions, and ξ be the number of bins in every dimension. The lower bound of the precision for HA, denoted as $\underline{Precision}$, for the IkNN query can be defined by Eq. (4.8).*

$$\underline{Precision} = 1 - \left(1 - \frac{1}{\xi}\right)^d.$$ (4.8)

Proof. Based on the above discussion that $Precision = 1 - P_{FN}$, we can derive that the lower bound of the precision for the IkNN query, that is, $\underline{Precision} = 1 - \overline{P}_{FN} = 1 - (1 - \frac{1}{\xi})^d$. Therefore, Eq. (4.8) holds. The proof completes.   □

4.2.3   LOCAL SKYBAND PRUNING FOR TOP-k DOMINATING QUERIES ON INCOMPLETE DATA

As analyzed in Section 4.1.3, the dominant cost for answering the top-k dominating (TKD) query on incomplete data is score computation. Hence, one of the feasible and effective ideas is to reduce the size of candidate objects, and thereby minimize the total cost of score computation for the candidate objects.

Fortunately, it is not difficult to observe that the objects with observed attributes falling inside the same set of dimensions actually satisfy the transitive dominance relationship. To this end, we reorganize the objects into buckets. Here, each bucket corresponds to a given subset of d' ($\leq d$) dimensions, and it accommodates all the objects whose observed attributes fall in those d' dimensions exactly. Accordingly, we present the *local skyband technique* to answer the TKD query over incomplete data. Here, the concept of k-skyband (kSB) query on incomplete data [Gao et al., 2014] is borrowed. The kSB query is a variant of skyline queries, and it retrieves the objects dominated by less than k objects. Since the objects within the same bucket share the same bit vector (i.e., the same missing dimension set), they can be regarded as a complete dataset in d'-dimensional space with $d' \leq d$. If we perform a kSB query for each bucket, the kSB query results collectively form a candidate set for a TKD query, as stated in Lemma 4.9.

Lemma 4.9 **(Local skyband pruning).** *Given an incomplete dataset $\mathbb{D}$, let bucket O_b represent the set of objects $o \in \mathbb{D}$ sharing the same bit vector b, i.e., $O_b = \{o \in \mathbb{D} \mid \beta_o = b\}$, and S_S be the local skyband object set returned by a k-skyband query over O_b. For an object $o \in O_b$, if o is not included in S_S, o cannot be returned by the TKD query on S, i.e., $o \notin S_S \Rightarrow o \notin S_G$.*

Proof. By contradiction. Assume that there is an object $o' \in O_b$ with $o' \notin S_S$ but $o' \in S_G$. As $o' \notin S_S$, o' is dominated by at least k objects from the bucket O_b, denoted as $D_{o'}$ with $|D_{o'}| \geq k$. Since the dominance relationship over the objects inside the same bucket satisfies transitivity, the objects dominated by o' are also dominated by all the objects in $D_{o'}$. In other words, all the objects in $D_{o'}$ dominate more objects than o', and thus, they all have higher scores than o'. Since $|D_{o'}| \geq k$, it is confirmed that $o' \notin S_G$, which contradicts with our assumption. Thus, our assumption is invalid. The proof completes. $\square$

Algorithm 4.4 Extended Skyband Based Algorithm (ESB)

Input: an incomplete dataset $\mathbb{D}$, a parameter k
Output: the result set S_G of a TKD query on $\mathbb{D}$
/* $kSB(O)$: the result set of a k-skyband query on a bucket O. */

1: initialize sets $S_C \leftarrow S_G \leftarrow \varnothing$
2: **for all** object $o \in \mathbb{D}$ **do**
3:     insert o into a bucket O based on β_o (create O if necessary)
4: **end for**
5: **for all** bucket O **do**
6:     $S_C \leftarrow S_C \bigcup kSB(O)$
7: **end for**
8: **for all** object $o \in S_C$ **do**
9:     update score(o) by comparing o with all the objects in $\mathbb{D}$
10: **end for**
11: add the k objects in S_C having the highest scores to S_G
12: **return** S_G

On top of the candidate set formed based on Lemma 4.9, we propose ESB algorithm with its pseudo-code depicted in Algorithm 4.4. ESB adopts the pruning-and-filtering paradigm to tackle the TKD query on incomplete data. It first partitions objects $o \in \mathbb{D}$ into its corresponding bucket based on its β_o (lines 2–4) and then performs a local kSB query for objects within the same bucket (lines 5–7). The collection of the returned results from kSB queries form a candidate set S_C to complete the pruning step. Next, the filtering step starts. ESB ranks the candidates in S_C based on their score values and returns the top-k candidates with the highest scores as the final query result (lines 8–12). Example 4.10 illustrates how ESB algorithm works.

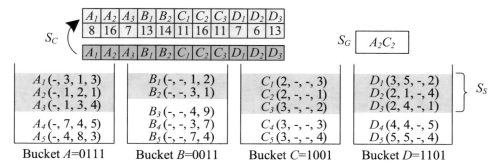

Figure 4.12: Example of local skyband pruning.

Example 4.10 Assume ESB algorithm is invoked for a top-k dominating query ($k = 2$) over our sample dataset shown in Figure 4.7, with the processing steps illustrated in Figure 4.12. It first clusters the objects into buckets based on their bit vectors. For instance, when the first object B_3 in Figure 4.7 is evaluated, a bucket B corresponding to the bit vector, ($\beta_{B_3} = 0011$), is created, and B_3 is the first object enrolled. In total, four buckets are created with each having five objects, as depicted in Figure 4.12. Note that, it is a coincidence that there are five objects in each of the four buckets. Then, it performs local 2-skyband queries on the objects within every bucket, with the local 2-skyband objects returned by each bucket, denoted as S_s, highlighted in Figure 4.12. Four sets of local 2-skyband objects form the candidate set S_C that contains 11 objects, with $S_C = \{A_1, A_2, A_3, B_1, B_2, C_1, C_2, C_3, D_1, D_2, D_3\}$. For these 11 objects in S_C, we then derive their scores based on the numbers of objects in S they dominate. As shown in Figure 4.12, objects A_2 and C_2 share the same highest score (i.e., 16), and thus, they are returned as the final result (i.e., S_G) of the top-k dominating query ($k = 2$).

4.2.4 UPPER BOUND SCORE PRUNING FOR TOP-k DOMINATING QUERIES ON INCOMPLETE DATA

From another angle, in order to minimize the candidate object size, we also attempt to integrate the ranking process of the top-k dominating query into the object evaluation, enabling an early termination of top-k dominating query processing before evaluating all the candidates.

Based on this intention, we present the concept of *upper bound score* that returns the maximum number of objects that a specified object o dominates, i.e., the upper bound of $\mathsf{score}(o)$, as stated in Lemma 4.11 below.

Lemma 4.11 **(Upper bound score)**. *Given an object $o \in \mathbb{D}$, let $T_i(o)$ be the maximum set of the objects p dominated by o on the i-th dimension. Formally, $T_i(o)$ can be defined as*

$$T_i(o) = \begin{cases} \{p \in \mathbb{D} - \{o\} | o.[i] \le p.[i]\} \cup S_i & if\ i \in Iset(o) \\ \mathbb{D} & otherwise, \end{cases} \tag{4.9}$$

where S_i represents the set of the objects whose i-th dimensional values are missing, and $Iset(o)$ denotes the set of dimensions where o has observed values. Based on $T_i(o)$, the upper bound of $\mathsf{score}(o)$, denoted as $\mathsf{MaxScore}(o)$, could be derived by Eq. (4.10).

$$\mathsf{MaxScore}(o) = min\{|T_1(o)|, |T_2(o)|, \ldots, |T_d(o)|\}. \tag{4.10}$$

Proof. First, we prove that $|T_i(o)|$ is an upper bound score for an object $o \in \mathbb{D}$. On the one hand, for the case that $i \notin Iset(o)$, it is obvious that $|T_i(o)| (= |\mathbb{D}|)$ is an upper bound for $\mathsf{score}(o)$. On the other hand, if $i \in Iset(o)$, according to Eq. (4.9), the object set $T_i(o)$ contains all objects that are not better than o in the i-th dimension and all the objects with their i-th dimensional values missing. Based on Definition 3.6, $T_i(o)$ contains all the possible objects that have the potential to be dominated by o. Thus, $|T_i(o)|$ is an upper bound of $\mathsf{score}(o)$ for $i \in Iset(o)$. In summary, we can conclude that $|T_i(o)|$ is an upper bound for $\mathsf{score}(o)$. Then, it is easy to find that the minimum cardinality of $T_i(o)$ for $1 \le i \le d$ (i.e., $\mathsf{MaxScore}(o)$) is also an upper bound score for o. The proof completes. □

For ease of understanding, we illustrate how to derive $\mathsf{MaxScore}(B_3)$ for object B_3 in our sample dataset (shown in Figure 4.7). We first get $T_1(B_3) = T_2(B_3) = S$ because $B_3.[1]$ and $B_3.[2]$ are missing, $T_3(B_3) = \{A_4, A_5, B_5, C_1, C_2, C_3, C_4, C_5, D_1, D_2, D_3, D_4, D_5\}$, and $T_4(B_3) = \varnothing$. Then, $\mathsf{MaxScore}(B_3) = min\{|T_1(B_3)|, |T_2(B_3)|, |T_3(B_3)|, |T_4(B_3)|\} = 0$. It is worth noting that $\mathsf{MaxScore}$ can be calculated at $O(N \cdot \lg N)$ cost based on the B^+-tree structure, where N is the dataset cardinality. Based on the concept of $\mathsf{MaxScore}(o)$, a pruning strategy is developed, as stated in Heuristic 4.12, which serves as an *early termination condition* for top-k dominating query on incomplete data.

Heuristic 4.12   (Upper bound score pruning). Given a top-k dominating query on an incomplete dataset $\mathbb{D}$, let S_C be a candidate set containing k objects for the query and τ be the smallest score for all objects in S_C, i.e., $|S_C| = k$ and $\forall c \in S_C$, score$(c) \geq \tau$ and $\exists c' \in S_C$, score$(c') = \tau$. For a specified object $o \in \mathbb{D}$ with MaxScore$(o) \leq \tau$, it can be safely pruned away as it cannot be an actual answer object for the top-k dominating query over $\mathbb{D}$.

Proof. First, $\forall c \in S_C$, score$(c) \geq \tau$. Second, score$(o) \leq$ MaxScore$(o) \leq \tau$. Thus, $\forall c \in S_C$, score$(c) \geq$ score(o). As $|S_C| = k$, there are k objects having higher scores than o, and object o cannot be a real answer object for the top-k dominating query. □

Based on Heuristic 4.12, we develop UBB algorithm with its pseudo-code presented in Algorithm 4.5. It takes as inputs an incomplete dataset $\mathbb{D}$, a parameter k, and a priority queue F with all the objects $o \in \mathbb{D}$ sorted in *descending* order of their MaxScore(o). First of all, UBB initializes two sets S_C and S_G to empty, and sets τ as -1 (line 1). Here, τ is to record the minimum score of the objects in S_C, and it is set to -1 if the set S_C contains less than k objects. Then, it visits the objects in F one by one until F is empty or early termination condition is satisfied (lines 2–16). Specifically, UBB dequeues the top object o of F. If MaxScore$(o) \leq \tau$, the early termination condition of Heuristic 4.12 is satisfied, and the while-loop can be finished. Note that the condition MaxScore$(o) \leq \tau$ and objects in F are sorted in descending order of MaxScore to guarantee that object o and all the remaining objects in F have their scores bounded by τ. In addition, it also ensures that the candidate set S_C is full, and it contains k objects with their scores $\geq \tau \geq 0$. On the other hand, if the early termination condition is not satisfied, the evaluation continues (lines 6–15). UBB computes score(o) via a function Get-Score that derives score(o) based on pairwise comparisons (line 7). If τ is -1, the candidate set S_C is not full, and object o is enrolled into S_C (line 9). Otherwise, if score(o) is larger than τ, object o is also enrolled into S_C to replace the object $p \in S_C$ having the smallest score value (i.e., τ). τ is updated as well if S_C is updated (line 13).

Example 4.13   We illustrate UBB algorithm for a top-k dominating query ($k = 2$) on a sample dataset depicted in Figure 4.7, with the priority queue F over the sample dataset shown in Figure 4.13, which ranks the objects in the non-ascending order of the upper bound score values. First, the head object of F (object C_2 first and object A_2 second) is evaluated one by one, after which $S_C = \{C_2, A_2\}$ and $\tau = 16$. Then, the next dequeued object B_2 is evaluated. As MaxScore$(B_2) = 16$, the early termination condition is satisfied. Thus, $\{C_2, A_2\}$ is returned as the final result set of the top-k dominating query ($k = 2$) and terminates. □

Algorithm 4.5 Upper Bound Based Algorithm (UBB)

Input: an incomplete dataset $\mathbb{D}$, a parameter k, a pre-computed priority queue F sorting all objects from $\mathbb{D}$ in descending order of their MaxScore
Output: the result set S_G of a TKD query on $\mathbb{D}$

1: initialize sets $S_C \leftarrow S_G \leftarrow \varnothing$ and $\tau \leftarrow -1$
2: **while** F is not empty **do**
3:    $o \leftarrow$ de-queue(F)
4:    **if** MaxScore(o) $\leq \tau$ **then**
5:       **break**   // Heuristic 4.12
6:    **else**
7:       score(o) $\leftarrow$ Get-Score(o)
8:       **if** score(o) $> \tau$ or $\tau < 0$ **then**
9:          $S_C \leftarrow S_C \bigcup \{o\}$
10:          **if** $|S_C| > k$ **then**
11:             S_C $S_C - \{p\}$ with $p \in S_C$ and score(p)$=\tau$
12:          **end if**
13:          update $\tau \leftarrow \min\{\text{score}(c) \mid c \in S_C\}$ if $|S_C| = k$
14:       **end if**
15:    **end if**
16: **end while**
17: **return** $S_G \leftarrow S_C$

ID	C_2	A_2	B_2	B_1	C_3	D_3	A_1	C_1	C_4	D_1	A_5	A_3	B_5	C_5	D_2	D_5	A_4	D_4	B_4	B_3
MaxScore	19	17	16	15	15	15	12	12	12	12	10	8	8	8	8	8	3	3	1	0

Figure 4.13: The priority queue F for the dataset in Figure 4.7.

4.2.5   BITMAP PRUNING FOR TOP-k DOMINATING QUERIES ON INCOMPLETE DATA

The basic (and binned) bitmap index has been introduced in Section 4.1.3. Now we are going to explain how to leverage the *bitmap pruning* technique (on top of the basic bitmap index) to calculate the score of an object (stated in Definition 3.7) for answering top-k dominating query on incomplete data. Then, as a complement, we summarize the generalization of the bitmap pruning to the binned bitmap index and introduce the *partial score pruning* for supporting the top-k dominating query on incomplete data. Finally, we discuss the tradeoff between the storage cost and the search efficiency of the binned bitmap index for processing top-k dominating query on incomplete data.

To begin with, we introduce four object sets w.r.t. an object o, i.e., P, Q, $\Phi(o)$, and nonD(o). Specifically, Q denotes the set of objects, excluding object o, that are not better than

o or missing in the dimensions in $Iset(o)$; P is a subset of Q which refers to the set of objects that are strictly worse than o or missing on each dimension in $Iset(o)$; $\Phi(o)$ represents the set of objects that are incomparable to o; and $nonD(o)$ refers to the set of objects in $(Q - P)$ that are not dominated by o. For ease of understanding, the containment relationship of the sets P, Q, $\Phi(o)$, and $nonD(o)$ is plotted in Figure 4.14.

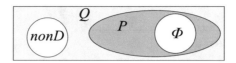

Figure 4.14: The Venn diagram of object sets P, Q, Φ, and $nonD$.

In the following, we first explain how the bitmap index can facilitate the computation of sets Q and P, as presented in Definition 4.14. It is important to note that both Q^i and P^i consist of the objects that might be dominated by o purely based on the values in the i-th dimension, and P^i is a subset of Q^i. In this book, for clarity, we represent the corresponding (*vertical*) bit-vectors encoding the object sets Q^i and P^i as $[Q^i]$ and $[P^i]$, respectively, which are abstracted from the bitmap index. Specifically, both $[Q^i]$ and $[P^i]$ have the length of $|\mathbb{D}|$ bits, with one bit corresponding to an object in $\mathbb{D}$. If an object is included in Q^i or P^i, the corresponding bit in $[Q^i]$ or $[P^i]$ is set to 1 in our bitmap index. Otherwise, the bit is set to 0.

Definition 4.14 (**Set computation**). Let $Q^i = P^i = \mathbb{D}$ if $o.[i]$ is missing; otherwise $Q^i = \{p \in \mathbb{D} \mid o.[i] \leq p.[i] \vee p.[i]$ is missing$\}$ and $P^i = \{p \in \mathbb{D} \mid o.[i] < p.[i] \vee p.[i]$ is missing$\}$, then sets Q and P are calculated as

$$Q = \bigcap_{i=1}^{d} Q^i - \{o\}, \qquad P = \bigcap_{i=1}^{d} P^i. \tag{4.11}$$

For instance, our sample dataset has 20 objects, and hence, the bit-vectors $[Q^i]$ and $[P^i]$ for a specified object o have 20 bits, with the first bit w.r.t. A_1, the second bit w.r.t. A_2, and so on. Take B_3 as an example. Its corresponding set $Q^3 = \{A_4, A_5, B_3, B_5, C_1, C_2, C_3, C_4, C_5, D_1, D_2, D_3, D_4, D_5\}$, and the corresponding bit-vector $[Q^3] = 00011001011111111111$. Thus, based on bit-vectors $[Q^i]$ and $[P^i]$ in the bitmap index, we can easily get sets Q and P by fast bit-wise operations (without comparing the real dimensional values).

In addition, we observe that set Q, which is formed at a small cost by bit-wise operations with the help of our bitmap index, provides another upper bound score $\mathsf{MaxBitScore}(o)$, as stated in Heuristic 4.15.

Heuristic 4.15 (**Bitmap pruning**). Given an incomplete dataset $\mathbb{D}$ and a candidate set S_C for a top-k dominating query containing k objects in $\mathbb{D}$, let τ be the minimum score of the objects in

S_C. For a specified object $o \in (\mathbb{D} - S_C)$ with $\mathsf{MaxBitScore}(o) = |Q| \leq \tau$, it can be pruned away safely since it cannot be a real answer object for the TKD query on S.

Proof. Given an object o with $\mathsf{score}(o) = \lambda$, there are λ objects dominated by o, denoted as $R = \{p^n \mid o \prec p^n, p^n \in \mathbb{D}, n = 1, \ldots, \lambda\}$. We can easily observe that $\forall p^n \in R, p^n \in Q$. Hence, R is a subset of Q, i.e., $R \subseteq Q$, and thereby, $\lambda = \mathsf{score}(o) = |R| \leq |Q| = \mathsf{MaxBitScore}(o) \leq \tau$. Consequently, we are certain that $\mathsf{score}(o) \leq \tau$ and the proof completes. □

Back to our example object B_3. We have $\bigcap_{i=1}^{4} Q^i = \{B_3\}$, and thus, $\mathsf{MaxBitScore}(B_3) = |Q| = |\bigcap_{i=1}^{4} Q^i - \{B_3\}| = 0$. If S_C has k objects with $\tau = 1$, object B_3 can be discarded safely based on Heuristic 4.15. It is worth noting that, compared with $\mathsf{MaxScore}(o)$, $\mathsf{MaxBitScore}(o)$ actually offers a tighter upper bound for $\mathsf{score}(o)$, i.e., $\mathsf{MaxBitScore}(o) \leq \mathsf{MaxScore}(o)$ as stated in Lemma 4.16. We also list these two upper bounds for our sample objects in Figure 4.15 for illustration purpose.

ID	C_2	A_2	B_2	B_1	C_3	D_3	A_1	C_1	C_4	D_1	A_5	A_3	B_5	C_5	D_2	D_5	A_4	D_4	B_4	B_3
MaxScore	19	17	16	15	15	15	12	12	12	12	10	8	8	8	8	8	3	3	1	0
MaxBitScore	19	17	16	15	13	15	10	12	10	9	5	8	4	7	8	4	1	3	1	0

Figure 4.15: Comparison between $\mathsf{MaxScore}$ and $\mathsf{MaxBitScore}$.

Lemma 4.16 *Given a TKD query on an incomplete dataset $\mathbb{D}$ and an object $o \in \mathbb{D}$, $\mathsf{MaxBitScore}(o) \leq \mathsf{MaxScore}(o)$.*

Proof. On the one hand, for each object $q \in Q$, the condition (i.e., $o.[i] \leq q.[i] \lor q.[i]$ is missing) holds for all the dimensions $i \in Iset(o)$ where $o.[i]$ is observed. Hence, we can get that $q \in T_i(o)$ for all the dimensions $i \in Iset(o)$. On the other hand, for the dimensions i' where $o.[i']$ is missing, $T_{i'}(o) = \mathbb{D}$ according to Eq. (4.9), and thus, we have $q \in T_{i'}(o)$. In a word, assume that $\min\{|T_1(o)|, |T_2(o)|, \ldots, |T_d(o)|\} = |T_t(o)|$, we have $q \in T_t(o)$. As a summary, for any $q \in Q$, we have $q \in T_t(o)$ and hence $Q \subseteq T_t(o)$. Thus, $\mathsf{MaxBitScore}(o) = |Q| \leq |T_t(o)| = \mathsf{MaxScore}(o)$. The proof completes. □

As we know, $\mathsf{score(o)} = |R|$ if set R contains the set of objects dominated by object o. Assume that we partition R into two disjoint subsets $\Gamma(o)$ and $\Lambda(o)$ such that $\Gamma(o) = P - \Phi(o)$, which includes all the objects o' that are *strictly worse* than o in all dimensions where both o and o' have observed values (i.e., $Iset(o) \cap Iset(o')$) and meanwhile are dominated by o, and set $\Lambda(o) = Q - P - \mathsf{nonD}(o)$, which consists of the objects o'' that share the same value as o in at least one dimension and meanwhile are dominated by o. Then, we have $\mathsf{score(o)} = |\Gamma(o)| + |\Lambda(o)| = |Q - \Phi(o) - \mathsf{nonD}(o)|$.

Accordingly, using the bitmap index, we describe the evaluation of each (incomplete) object in the dataset for answering top-k dominating query. Given an object o, $\mathsf{MaxScore}(o)$ is first calculated, and then one compares it with τ. If object o cannot be filtered by MaxScore(o), MaxBitScore(o) is computed. One should again compare it against τ. As MaxBitScore(o) represents a tighter upper bound of score(o), more unqualified objects are expected to be filtered out. If the object o is not filtered out by the upper bound score pruning (with MaxScore values) and the bitmap pruning (with MaxBitScore values), it is the qualified object. We need to derive its real score based on the equation score(o) $= |\Gamma(o)| + |\Lambda(o)| = |Q - \Phi(o) - \text{nonD}(o)|$.

BIG-Score implements score calculation based on bitmap index using score(o) $= |\Gamma(o)| + |\Lambda(o)|$, with its pseudo-code presented in Algorithm 4.6. First, before deriving the real score, it derives the upper bound MaxBitScore(o) and compares it with τ, the minimum score value of a candidate object (lines 1–2). If the filtering condition depicted in Heuristic 4.15 is satisfied, object o can be filtered out immediately without calculating its score (lines 3–4). Otherwise, the object passes the filtering, and we need to derive its real score based on $|\Gamma(o)| + |\Lambda(o)|$ (lines 5–14). To be more specific, it derives $\Gamma(o)$ (line 6) and $\Lambda(o)$ (lines 7–13). As mentioned earlier, $(Q - P)$ forms a candidate set for nonD(o), and hence, for objects $p \in (Q - P)$, BIG-Score checks each observed dimension i of o to find the objects with $p.[i] = o.[i]$. A counter $tagT$ is associated with every object $p \in (Q - P)$ to count the number of dimensions i such that $p.[i] = o.[i]$. In other words, objects $p \in (Q - P)$ with corresponding $tagT$ being equivalent to $|Iset(o) \cap Iset(p)|$ form nonD(o). Once nonD(o) is formed, $\Lambda(o)$ value is derived, and BIG-Score returns $|\Gamma(o)| + |\Lambda(o)|$ and stops.

Algorithm 4.6 Get-Score Algorithm for BIG (BIG-Score)

Input: a bitmap index, an object o, $\Phi(o)$, τ, S_C, k
Output: the score of o, i.e., score(o)

1: get $[P^i]$ and $[Q^i]$ of o for each $1 \leq i \leq d$ from bitmap index
2: $Q \leftarrow \bigcap_{i=1}^{d} Q^i - \{o\}$, MaxBitScore($o$) $\leftarrow |Q|$
3: **if** $|S_C| = k$ and MaxBitScore(o) $\leq \tau$ **then**
4:     **return** 0   // o is pruned away by Heuristic 4.15
5: **else**
6:     $P \leftarrow \bigcap_{i=1}^{d} P^i$, $\Gamma(o) \leftarrow P - \Phi(o)$
7:     **for all** pair of $\langle p, i \rangle \in (Q - P) \times Iset(o)$ **do**
8:         **if** $p.[i] = o.[i]$ **then**
9:             $p.tagT \leftarrow p.tagT + 1$
10:        **end if**
11:    **end for**
12:    nonD(o) $\leftarrow$ nonD(o) $\cup \{p \in (Q - P) \mid p.tagT = |\beta_p \ \& \ \beta_o|\}$
13:    $\Lambda(o) \leftarrow Q - P - \text{nonD}(o)$
14: **end if**
15: **return** score(o) $\leftarrow |\Gamma(o)| + |\Lambda(o)|$

Example 4.17   We illustrate how the algorithm (that leverages BIG-Score) answers a T2D query issued on our sample dataset. Suppose the corresponding priority queue F and the bitmap index are ready, as shown in Figure 4.13 and Figure 4.8, respectively. In addition, Φ is available with $\forall o \in \mathbb{D}$, $\Phi(o) = \varnothing$. The algorithm starts its evaluation by continuously en-queueing the head entry from F. First, object C_2 is evaluated, and its C_2's score is calculated. Specifically, the corresponding bit vectors of C_2 from the bitmap index (depicted in Figure 4.8) are depicted as follows.

$$[P^1] = 1111111110011110011, \quad [P^2] = 11111111111111111111,$$
$$[P^3] = 11111111111111111111, \quad [P^4] = 10111101111011111011,$$

$$[Q^1] = 11111111111111111111, \quad [Q^2] = 11111111111111111111,$$
$$[Q^3] = 11111111111111111111, \quad [Q^4] = 11111111111111111111.$$

Since the candidate set $|S_C| = 0$, it then computes $\bigcap_{i=1}^{4}[Q^i] = 1111111111\,1111111111$, $[P] = \bigcap_{i=1}^{4}[P^i] = 1011110111001110\,011$, and sets $|\Gamma(C_2)| = |P - \Phi(C_2)| = |P| = 14$. Next, the algorithm examines the objects in $Q - P = \{A_2, B_2, C_1, D_2, D_3\}$. Among those objects, the subset $\{A_2, B_2, D_3\}$ forms nonD(C_2), because they are all the objects in $Q - P$, which are not dominated by C_2. Thereafter, $|\Lambda(C_2)| = |Q - P - \text{nonD}(C_2)| = 2$, and score$(C_2) = |\Gamma(C_2)| + |\Lambda(C_2)| = 14 + 2 = 16$. Object C_2 is then enrolled into a candidate set S_C. Next, object A_2 is evaluated. Similarly, score$(A_2) = 16$, and A_2 is enrolled to S_C. Now, $|S_C| = 2$ and $\tau = 16$. Then, object B_2 is evaluated. As MaxScore$(B_2) = 16$ which is the same as τ, the algorithm terminates early according to Heuristic 4.12. Finally, the result set $\{C_2, A_2\}$ of the top-k dominating query ($k = 2$) is returned. □

Generalization to the Binned Bitmap Index

We have now finished elaborating how to answer the top-k dominating query based on the *basic* bitmap index with the support of the bitmap pruning and the derived equation of score computation. Now, we describe the generalization of the presented techniques on top of the basic bitmap index to the binned bitmap index in order to solve the top-k dominating query on incomplete data.

First, due to the usage of the binning strategy, the object set encoded by the vertical bit-vector $[Q^i]$ (abstracted from the binned bitmap index) is a bit different. In the binned bitmap index, given an object o, if $o.[i]$ is observed, set $[Q^i]$ encodes all the objects that are located in the same bin as $o.[i]$.

Second, the bitmap pruning presented in Heuristic 4.15 is still applicable to the binned bitmap index, whereas the statement MaxBitScore$(o) \leq$ MaxScore(o) presented in Lemma 4.16 is no longer valid. Consequently, the filtering based on MaxBitScore(o) under binned bitmap index might not be able to achieve a good pruning power.

As an alternative, we develop a new *partial score pruning* heuristic, as presented in Heuristic 4.18, to help prune away certain unqualified objects.

Heuristic 4.18   **(Partial score pruning).** Given a top-k dominating query over an incomplete dataset $\mathbb{D}$ and a candidate set S_C containing k objects, let τ be the smallest score for all objects in S_C. For a specified object $o \in (\mathbb{D} - S_C)$, if $|\mathsf{nonD}(o)| > |Q| - |\Phi(o)| - \tau$, the object o can be discarded safely.

Proof. The proof is intuitive and skipped to save space.   □

Last but not least, the score computation (as well as the top-k dominating query) on top of the binned bitmap index shares the same flow as that on top of the basic bitmap index. It first implements the filtering step based on Heuristic 4.15. If object o cannot be filtered, its score $\mathsf{score}(o)$ has to be derived based on $|\Gamma(o)| + |\Lambda(o)|$ in the similar way. In particular, during forming $\mathsf{nonD}(o)$, it implements Heuristic 4.18. In addition, it is worth pointing out that, in order to get the score of an object o, we utilize B^+-trees in our implementation to get the set $\mathsf{nonD}(o)$ quickly and to avoid unqualified checks. However, the usage of B^+-trees is optional, which depends on the tradeoff between extra space cost and enhanced efficiency.

Discussion

As mentioned earlier, the number of bins in the i-th dimension (i.e., ξ value) has a direct impact on the performance of the algorithm based on the binned bitmap index for the top-k dominating query on incomplete data. In the following, we present an analytical model to analyze the space cost and query processing cost affected by ξ and discuss how to select a proper ξ value to optimize the *space-time* tradeoff for the algorithm based on the binned bitmap index. For ease of analysis, let N, d, and σ be the cardinality, the dimensionality, and the missing rate of the dataset, respectively. Then, the space cost, denoted as $cost_s$, is the size of the binned bitmap index, formally,

$$cost_s = N \times (\xi + 1) \times d. \tag{4.12}$$

On the other hand, the query cost, denoted as $cost_t$, can be approximated by the cost incurred to form set $\mathsf{nonD}(o)$, as stated in Eq. (4.13). The reason is that the score calculation based on $|Q - \Phi(o) - \mathsf{nonD}(o)|$ relies on Q, $\Phi(o)$, and $\mathsf{nonD}(o)$. Given the fact that Q can be formed by fast bit-operations and $\Phi(o)$ is an input, the cost of score calculation is mainly contributed by the formation of set $\mathsf{nonD}(o)$. In addition, score calculation is the most expensive operation in the top-k dominating query processing, and its cost dominates the main query cost.

$$cost_t = d \times \left(\log(\sigma N) + \left\lceil \frac{\sigma N}{\xi} \right\rceil - 1 \right). \tag{4.13}$$

In particular, for an object o that cannot be pruned away, the set $\mathsf{nonD}(o)$ is formed in order to obtain its real score. However, the cost of getting $\mathsf{nonD}(o)$ is related to the value of

ξ. In our implementation, for each observed dimension of o, we need to traverse the B$^+$-tree to locate the minimum boundary of the bin where o is located, which takes $\log(\sigma N)$ cost. To further validate whether all the objects located in this bin are worse than o in this dimension, we need to access $(\lceil \sigma N/\xi \rceil - 1)$ key values via the sequential scanning in B$^+$-tree in the worst case. Consider that, in the worst case, we need to traverse all the B$^+$-trees, and thus, the total cost is $d \times (\log(\sigma N) + \lceil \sigma N/\xi \rceil - 1)$.

Based on Eq. (4.12) and Eq. (4.13), we can find that as the value of ξ grows, the space saving is reduced and the query processing cost drops. This is because when ξ ascends, the range of dimensional values captured by every bin becomes small, and the average key value size (i.e., $\lceil \sigma N/\xi \rceil - 1$) visited by the search algorithm in every B^+ tree becomes small. In an extreme case when ξ is set to the number of distinct dimensional values (i.e., $\xi = C + 1$), the binned bitmap index is the same as the bitmap index.

In other words, a small ξ value can help to cut down the index size efficiently, but the query cost is increased. Hence, we cannot minimize both the index size and the query processing cost simultaneously. As both the space cost and the query cost are important performance metrics, and they both are affected by ξ, we consider the product of those two costs as the main cost, as shown in Eq. (4.14).

$$
\begin{aligned}
cost &= cost_s \times cost_t \\
&= N \cdot (\xi + 1) \cdot d^2 \cdot \left(\log(\sigma N) + \left\lceil \frac{\sigma N}{\xi} \right\rceil - 1 \right) \quad (4.14) \\
\xi &= \sqrt{\frac{\sigma N}{\log(\sigma N) - 1}}. \quad (4.15)
\end{aligned}
$$

Note that some existing works have also adopted the same equation to analyze the cost [Wu et al., 2010]. Therefore, in order to optimize the tradeoff between space cost and query cost, we try to minimize $cost$, i.e., we set the derivative of $cost$ to be zero and obtain the optimal value of ξ as depicted in Eq. (4.15). As an example, for N =100,000 and $\sigma = 0.1$, we can get the optimal bin size $\xi = 29$. When N =16,000 and $\sigma = 0.2$, the optimal bin size ξ is 17.

4.3   CROWDSOURCING TECHNIQUES

Collective intelligence has become a hot topic with the development of Web 3.0 and the emerging of artificial intelligence (AI) techniques. As a consequence, many crowdsourcing plat-forms [Yuen et al., 2011] have appeared, such as Amazon Mechanical Turk (AMT),[3] Crowd-flower,[4] and Upwork,[5] each of which acts as an intermediary between the requesters and the workers. Over the crowdsourcing platforms, the requester posts a series of tasks, and the workers

---

[3]Available at https://www.mturk.com/mturk/.
[4]Available at https://www.crowdflower.com.
[5]Available at https://www.upwork.com.

answer those tasks and get paid. Compared with conventional trade markets, the crowdsourcing platform offers a more free employment contract where workers can come and go as they wish.

Incomplete data is ubiquitous in a wide spectrum of real-life applications, such as sensor network, data integration, privacy preservation, etc. Incomplete data queries have been extensively explored in the past decade, including skyline queries [Khalefa et al., 2008, Miao et al., 2016d], top-k queries [Haghani et al., 2009, Soliman et al., 2010], similarity queries [Cheng et al., 2014, Cuzzocrea and Nucita, 2011, Miao et al., 2016c], and so on. Nonetheless, most of the existing models and approaches for incomplete data queries only rely on machine power. As well known, the machine has limitations in some cases where the human is powerful [Franklin et al., 2011].

The skyline query (over complete data) finds the objects that are not worse than other objects in all attributes, and better than them in at least one attribute. It has a large application base in many real-life scenarios such as decision making, profile-based recommendation, location-based services, and so forth. Take a movie recommendation system dataset depicted in Table 4.1 as example. It contains five movies (i.e., objects) $\{o_1, o_2, o_3, o_4, o_5\}$ with ratings from five audiences (w.r.t. attributes) $\{a_1, a_2, a_3, a_4, a_5\}$. In this dataset, some ratings are missing. For instance, the object o_2's value on the attribute a_2 is missing, and thus, it is denoted by the variable $Var(o_2, a_2)$. When the skyline query is finding the movies that have no lower rating than any other object from each audience, it is not able to get the real query result objects due to the incomplete dataset.

Table 4.1: A sample dataset for crowd skyline queries

ID	Name	Film Ratings from Audiences				
		a_1	a_2	a_3	a_4	a_5
o_1	Schindler's List (1993)	5	2	3	4	1
o_2	Se7en (1995)	6	$Var(o_2; a_2)$	2	2	2
o_3	The Godfather (1972)	1	1	$Var(o_3; a_3)$	5	3
o_4	The Lion King (1994)	4	3	1	2	1
o_5	Star Wars (1977)	5	$Var(o_5; a_2)$	$Var(o_5; a_3)$	$Var(o_5; a_4)$	1

Therefore, we resort to crowdsourcing techniques to solve the queries over incomplete dataset. We explore in which order the tasks should be posted so as to benefit the query requester in terms of query quality and crowd cost. To this end, we present a robust framework, termed as BayesCrowd, for the crowd skyline queries on incomplete data. In particular, BayesCrowd takes into account the data correlation in processing incomplete data, which is not supported by almost all the previous work on querying incomplete data, such as Cheng et al. [2014], Khalefa et al. [2008], and Miao et al. [2016d].

4.3.1   CROWDSOURCING FRAMEWORK FOR SKYLINE QUERIES ON INCOMPLETE DATA

The crowd skyline problem is faced with three big challenges: (i) how to capture data correlation, (ii) how to represent query result objects, and (iii) how to prioritize the crowd tasks. As long as these questions are answered satisfactorily, the framework BayesCrowd will work well (even for any type of queries over incomplete data).

First, we train the Bayesian network over data attributes in order to capture data correlation. Then, with the help of the trained Bayesian network, we obtain the probability distribution of the missing values on every data attribute. Second, in BayesCrowd, we leverage a typical incomplete database representation model [Imieliński and Lipski Jr, 1984], i.e., *c-table*, to assign each object a condition of becoming a query answer. The object's condition is a boolean combination of inequalities involving missing values (i.e., variables) and constants. The probability of the condition being satisfied is equal to the possibility of the corresponding object being a query answer. Simply speaking, the object is not a query answer if its condition is not satisfied. Third, BayesCrowd supports crowdsourcing the most beneficial tasks with budget constraints. We introduce a *marginal utility function* to measure the benefit of crowdsourcing an expression (i.e., the task) in the condition for answering crowd queries. The marginal utility function is defined based on the probability of the object being a query answer. BayesCrowd integrates a high-accuracy strategy for the crowd task selection, which also takes into account budget and latency tradeoff.

In particular, during crowd task selection, one has to obtain the marginal utility via leveraging the probability of the object being a query answer. Nevertheless, the probability computation is computationally infeasible (at least as hard as #SAT problem). To this end, we propose an adaptive DPLL (i.e., Davis–Putnam–Logemann–Loveland) (ADPLL for short) algorithm to accelerate computation. Specifically, it recursively selects the most frequent variables to assign a possible value, which reduces the expression correlation as quickly as possible. It yields high efficiency in probability computation, because the probability of the condition with independent expressions can be derived directly.

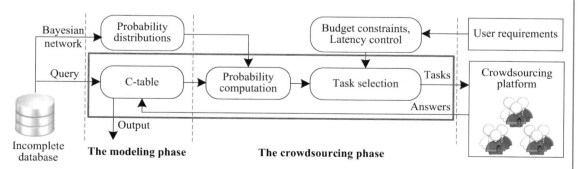

Figure 4.16: The architecture of BayesCrowd.

As a result, BayesCrowd consists of two main phases including *the modeling phase* and *the crowdsourcing phase*. The first phase is to model each data object with a condition of being a query answer, which makes the preparation for the next phase. In the crowdsourcing phase, BayesCrowd selects the tasks for crowdsourcing for achieving the goal of maximizing the requester's benefit. Figure 4.16 illustrates the framework of BayesCrowd. In the preprocessing step, it trains the Bayesian network over the dataset in order to capture the data correlation. Then, using the trained Bayesian network, it learns the probability distribution of the missing values on each attribute, which is an input of BayesCrowd. In the modeling phase, the query result objects are represented under the c-table model. This is the preparation for the crowd task selection at the next phase. When BayesCrowd enters the crowdsourcing step, it takes into account the users' requirements (e.g., budget constraints and latency control). It selects tasks for crowdsourcing based on a marginal utility function of the requester.

Algorithm 4.7 BayesCrowd Framework

Input: an incomplete dataset $\mathcal{O}$, a query Q
Output: a query result set $\mathcal{R}$

1: $\mathcal{C} \longleftarrow$ Get-CTable($\mathcal{O}, Q$)
2: select the crowd tasks $\mathcal{T}$ based on a marginal utility function
3: post tasks $\mathcal{T}$ on a crowdsourcing platform
4: collect answers from the crowd workers
5: derive a query result set $\mathcal{R}$
6: **return** $\mathcal{R}$

Algorithm 4.7 depicts the general procedure of BayesCrowd. It takes as inputs an incomplete dataset $\mathcal{O}$ (with the learned probability distributions) and a query Q, and outputs a query result set $\mathcal{R}$. First, in the modeling phase, BayesCrowd constructs the c-table, denoted as $\mathcal{C}$, for the query Q via recalling the function Get-CTable (line 1). Then, BayesCrowd enters the second phase. It selects the awaiting crowd tasks based on an objective function (i.e., the requester's marginal utility function). Next, those selected tasks are posted on crowdsourcing markets (lines 2–3). Thereafter, it receives the task answers from the crowd workers and infers the query result set $\mathcal{R}$ (lines 4–5). Finally, BayesCrowd returns $\mathcal{R}$, and terminates (line 6).

Preprocessing

In order to consider data correlation during processing incomplete data, we assume that every attribute in the dataset follows a certain probability distribution.

Specifically, we train the Bayesian network on the dataset by using Banjo.[6] Banjo is a software application and framework for *structure learning* of static and dynamic Bayesian networks, and it is implemented in Java language. Then, we estimate the network structure parameters via

---

[6]Available at https://users.cs.duke.edu/~amink/software/banjo/.

recalling Infer.Net,[7] which is a framework for running Bayesian inference in graphical models, and is implemented in C# language. Once we have the Bayesian network, we infer the probability distribution (i.e., the probability mass function) of the missing values on each attribute by leveraging Bayes rules.

We devote the rest of this chapter to the c-table construction and the probability computation of the conditions in the c-table, respectively. Finally, we elaborate the crowdsourcing phase of BayesCrowd.

4.3.2 C-TABLE CONSTRUCTION

The *c-table* model was first proposed by the foundational research work of Imieliński and Lipski Jr [1984]. It is formalized in Definition 4.19. Here, we expect to utilize the *c-table* model to represent the skyline objects over incomplete dataset.

Definition 4.19 (**c-table**) [Green and Tannen, 2006, Imieliński and Lipski Jr, 1984]. A *conditional database*, or *c-table* for short, is a tuple $CD = \langle R_1, \cdots, R_k, \Phi \rangle$, in which $\langle R_1, \cdots, R_k \rangle$ is a relational database instance, and Φ assigns a propositional formula Φ_t to every tuple t in each relation $R_1, \cdots, R_k$. Given a valuation θ of the variable in Φ, the *world associated with* θ is $W^\theta = \langle R_1^\theta, \cdots, R_k^\theta \rangle$, where $R_i^\theta = \{t \mid t \in R_i, \Phi_t[\theta] = true\}$ for $i = 1, \cdots, k$.

Example 4.20 For the skyline query on the sample dataset shown in Table 4.1, its c-table (i.e., the object-condition pairs) is depicted in Table 4.2. The conditions of o_2 and o_3 are true. It means that o_2 and o_3 are definitely the result objects of the skyline query. In addition, the condition of o_1, i.e., $\phi(o_1) = (Var(o_5, a_2) < 2) \vee (Var(o_5, a_3) < 3) \vee (Var(o_5, a_4) < 4)$. It indicates that if $\phi(o_1)$ is satisfied, then o_1 is a skyline result object. In other words, the probability of $\phi(o_1)$ (being satisfied) is equivalent to the possibility of the object o_1 being a skyline result object.

Table 4.2: The c-table over the sample dataset

Object	Condition
o_1	$(Var(o_5; a_2) < 2) \vee (Var(o_5; a_3) < 3) < (Var(o_5; a_4) < 4)$
o_2	True
o_3	True
o_4	$(Var(o_2; a_2) < 3) \wedge [(Var(o_5; a_2) < 3) \vee (Var(o_5; a_3) < 1) \vee (Var(o_5; a_4) < 2)]$
o_5	$[(Var(o_5; a_2) > 2) \vee (Var(o_5; a_3) > 3) \vee (Var(o_5; a_4) > 4)] \wedge [(Var(o_5; a_2) > Var(o_2; a_2)) \vee (Var(o_5; a_3) > 2) \vee (Var(o_5; a_4) > 2)]$

---

[7]Available at http://infernet.azurewebsites.net/.

As shown in Figure 4.16, in the modeling phase, BayesCrowd constructs the c-table for the query Q. In the following, we carefully explain how to obtain the c-table (i.e., the conditions in the c-table) efficiently. In addition, it is important to note that when the query results are represented under the c-table model with *conditions*, the probability of an object o's condition, denoted as $\phi(o)$, being satisfied indicates the possibility of the object o being a skyline query result object. Without loss of generality, in this book, we call the inequality in the condition an *expression*. It corresponds to the crowd task for crowdsourcing.

Deriving the Dominator Set

First, let us make an analysis. For the skyline query, an object o is a query answer if it is not dominated by any other object in the dataset. In other words, the condition of o being an answer object is to have at least one better attribute value for o than the objects that probably dominate o.

For an object $o \in \mathcal{O}$, let $\mathcal{D}(o)$ be the set of all the objects that are likely to dominate o on the incomplete dataset. For simplicity, we call it *the dominator set* of o throughout this chapter. Then, the condition of o, i.e., $\phi(o)$, consists of $|\mathcal{D}(o)|$ conjuncts, and each of the conjuncts encompasses at most d disjuncts, where d is the number of data attributes. Without loss of generality, in this book, the disjunct is usually called the expression/task, which is an inequality between a variable and a constant or between two variables.

As an example, if a dominator set $\mathcal{D}(o) = \{o_1, o_2, \cdots\}$, the condition of o, i.e., $\phi(o)$, can be formulated as $[o_1 \nprec o] \land [o_2 \nprec o] \land \cdots$. In particular, the conjunct $o_1 \nprec o$ is denoted as the disjunction of at most d expressions, e.g., $[o.[1] > o_1.[1]] \lor \cdots \lor [o.[d] > o_1.[d]]$. Here, it is assumed that, the larger the attribute value, the better. Consequently, the condition in this book is represented in CNF form.

Naturally, there appears another question along with the analysis, i.e., how to derive $\mathcal{D}(o)$ efficiently. This is because, upon the dominator set $\mathcal{D}(o)$ being obtained, the condition of o can be easily derived in CNF form. In light of this, we define the dominator set $\mathcal{D}(o)$, as stated in Definition 4.21, in order to further decompose the mission of the dominator set derivation.

Definition 4.21   (The dominator set). Given a skyline query over an incomplete dataset $\mathcal{O}$, for each object $o \in \mathcal{O}$, the dominator set $\mathcal{D}(o)$ (consisting of all the objects that possibly dominate o) can be derived by Eq. (4.16), in which d is the number of data attributes and O_i represents the set of the objects whose i-th dimensional values are missing.

$$\mathcal{D}(o) = \bigcap_{i=1}^{d} D_i(o) \tag{4.16}$$

$$D_i(o) = \begin{cases} \{p \in \mathcal{O} - \{o\} \mid o.[i] \leq p.[i]\} \cup O_i & \text{if } o.[i] \quad \text{is observed} \\ \mathcal{O} - \{o\} & \text{otherwise.} \end{cases} \tag{4.17}$$

The set $D_i(o)$ is composed of a group of the objects whose i-th attribute values are missing or not worse than that of o, if o has an observed value in attribute i. Otherwise, if o misses its value in the attribute i, $D_i(o)$ is set as the super set $(\mathcal{O} - \{o\})$. Hence, the intersection set of $D_i(o)$s ($i = 1, \cdots, d$) contains the objects that are missing or not worse than o in each attribute, which definitely includes all the objects that have the possibilities to dominate o, i.e., forming the dominator set $\mathcal{D}(o)$. For ease of understanding, Table 4.3 lists the dominator set for every object over our sample dataset (depicted in Table 4.1).

Table 4.3: The dominator sets for the objects on the sample dataset

Object	o_1	o_2	o_3	o_4	o_5
$\mathcal{D}$	$\{o_5\}$	$\varnothing$	$\varnothing$	$\{o_2, o_5\}$	$\{o_1, o_2\}$

It is worth pointing out that the set $D_i(o)$ can be efficiently derived via a B^+-tree index on the i-th attribute. In addition, in implementation, the intersection set of those D_i sets defined in Eq. (4.16) is computed through the fast bit-wise operation [Colantonio and Di Pietro, 2010, Wu et al., 2010].

Getting the C-Table
Combining the techniques of deriving the dominator set, we propose an efficient algorithm for c-table construction.

Algorithm 4.8 depicts the procedure of constructing c-table for a skyline query. It takes as inputs an incomplete dataset $\mathcal{O}$, a query Q, and a pruning threshold α, and outputs a c-table, denoted as $\mathcal{C}$. To begin with, it initializes $\mathcal{C}$ as an empty set (line 1). Then, for each object $o \in \mathcal{O}$, it derives its dominator set $\mathcal{D}(o)$ based on Definition 4.21 (line 3). Note that, the B^+-tree indexes and the bit-wise operation are employed to accelerate $\mathcal{D}(o)$ derivation. If there is no object in $\mathcal{D}(o)$, it indicates that the object o is certainly a skyline point. Hence, in this case, the condition $\phi(o)$ is assigned as the value of *true* (lines 4–5). On the contrary, if there are a large fraction of objects in the dominator set $\mathcal{D}(o)$, signifying a lot of objects are possible to dominate o, as a result, we use a threshold α to identify the case that o is very likely to be dominated. If $|\mathcal{D}(o)| > \alpha \cdot |\mathcal{O}|$, we deem o is not a skyline point, and set $\phi(o)$ as the value of *false* (lines 7–8). Otherwise, we generate the condition $\phi(o)$ using the dominator set $\mathcal{D}(o)$ (line 10). Specifically, if there exists an object $o' \in \mathcal{D}(o)$ dominating o, then o is not a skyline point, and thus, the condition $\phi(o)$ is set as *false* (lines 11–12). Whatever the condition $\phi(o)$ is, it is added to a c-table $\mathcal{C}$ (line 16). Finally, the algorithm stops after returning the c-table $\mathcal{C}$ (line 18).

It is worth mentioning that the parameter α is necessary to prune the case that o is very likely to be dominated. On the one hand, when $\mathcal{D}(o)$ is large, (i.e., o is probably dominated by too many objects), the probability of o being a query result object is near zero. On the other hand,

---

Algorithm 4.8 Get-CTable

Input: an incomplete dataset $\mathcal{O}$, a query Q, a pruning threshold α
Output: a c-table $\mathcal{C}$

1: $\mathcal{C} \longleftarrow \varnothing$
2: **for all** object $o \in \mathcal{O}$ **do**
3:     derive its dominator set $\mathcal{D}(o)$ using Eq. (4.16)
4:     **if** $|\mathcal{D}(o)| = 0$ **then**
5:        $\phi(o) \longleftarrow true$ // o is a skyline point
6:     **else**
7:        **if** $|\mathcal{D}(o)| > \alpha \cdot |\mathcal{O}|$ **then**
8:           $\phi(o) \longleftarrow false$ // o is deemed not to be a skyline point
9:        **else**
10:          generate the condition $\phi(o)$ of o in CNF form
11:          **if** $\exists o' \in \mathcal{D}(o)$ dominates o **then**
12:             $\phi(o) \longleftarrow false$ // o is not a skyline point
13:          **end if**
14:       **end if**
15:    **end if**
16:    $\mathcal{C} \longleftarrow \mathcal{C} + \{\langle o, \phi(o)\rangle\}$
17: **end for**
18: **return** $\mathcal{C}$

---

a large set of $\mathcal{D}(o)$ results in a complex condition $\phi(o)$ (that contains too many conjuncts), which hinders significantly the probability computation of $\Pr(\phi(o))$. Nevertheless, even though it gets the probability of the complex condition, it brings limited benefit to the crowdsourcing mission of BayesCrowd. In other words, what you gain cannot compensate for what you pain. Hence, it is unnecessary to spend more cost in deriving the probability of those complex conditions. Moreover, it is easy to conclude that the smaller the value of α, the more efficient the probability computation. A big value of α degrades remarkably the efficiency of probability computation, yet very slightly improves the query accuracy or the requester's utility.

Example 4.22   For the skyline query over the sample dataset, we have shown the c-table and the dominator sets in Table 4.2 and Table 4.3, respectively. Here, we are going to explain how to get the conditions, based on the dominator sets. First, for the object o_1 (from the sample dataset depicted in Table 4.1), we could get $\mathcal{D}(o_1) = \{o_5\}$ (as shown in Table 4.3). It means that only the object o_5 has the possibility to dominate o_1. In other words, if o_1 defeats o_5 in at least one of the attributes, then o_5 would not dominate o_1, and thus, o_1 would be a skyline point. Therefore, the condition of o_1, i.e., $\phi(o_1)$, is written as $(Var(o_5, a_2) < 2) \vee (Var(o_5, a_3) < 3) \vee (Var(o_5, a_4) < 4)$, as depicted in Table 4.2.

Then, for the object o_2, we set the condition of o_2, i.e., $\phi(o_2)$, as true, due to $\mathcal{D}(o_2) = \varnothing$. It indicates that there is no object dominating o_2. Hence, the object o_2 is a skyline point. Similarly, we can derive that the condition $\phi(o_3)$ gets the value of true. The condition $\phi(o_4)$ is $(Var(o_2, a_2) < 3) \wedge [(Var(o_5, a_2) < 3) \vee (Var(o_5, a_3) < 1) \vee (Var(o_5, a_4) < 2)]$. The condition $\phi(o_5)$ is $[(Var(o_5, a_2) > 2) \vee (Var(o_5, a_3) > 3) \vee (Var(o_5, a_4) > 4)] \wedge [(Var(o_5, a_2) > Var(o_2, a_2)) \vee (Var(o_5, a_3) > 2) \vee (Var(o_5, a_4) > 2)]$, as shown in Table 4.2.

Let $|\mathcal{O}|$ be the dataset cardinality, and d be the number of attributes in the dataset. The complexity of c-table construction is $O(|\mathcal{O}| \cdot (d \cdot |\mathcal{O}| \lg |\mathcal{O}| + d \cdot |\mathcal{D}(o)|))$. Specifically, for every object o, the complexity of getting the dominator set $\mathcal{D}(o)$ is $O(d \cdot |\mathcal{O}| \lg |\mathcal{O}|)$. It results from deriving all the set D_is (as defined in Definition 4.21) over d attributes via leveraging the B^+-tree index on each attribute. Note that the bit-wise operation is employed to derive the intersection set of those D_i sets, which consumes a little overhead. In addition, generating the condition of the object o needs $O(d \cdot |\mathcal{D}(o)|)$ time, as every condition has $|\mathcal{D}(o)|$ conjuncts with each conjunct having at most d disjuncts (i.e., expressions).

4.3.3 PROBABILITY COMPUTATION

When we have gotten the c-table (conditions), we are ready to derive the probability $\Pr(\phi(o))$ of each condition $\phi(o)$, which is exactly the probability of the object o being a result object. In this part, we present a novel and efficient algorithm, called ADPLL, for probability computation.

An intuitive solution to compute $\Pr(\phi(o))$ is to evaluate all the variable value combinations (i.e., assignments) of the variables (w.r.t., missing values) in $\phi(o)$, and aggregate the probability of those assignments to get $\Pr(\phi(o))$. One can easily find that it is a #SAT problem[8] if the variables can only get the values of 0 or 1 randomly. The #SAT problem is also known as the (weighted) model counting problem [Gomes et al., 2008], which is a #P-complete problem. However, in our probability computation problem, the variables can get a group of values (not just the values of 0 or 1) under certain probability massive functions (pmfs). It signifies that our probability computation problem is at least as hard as the #SAT problem.

To this end, we resort to the solvers of the #SAT problem in order to address our problem efficiently. DPLL search [Sang et al., 2005, Thiffault et al., 2004] is a popular and efficient solver for the #SAT problem, which is able to derive the accurate probability of the formula for the case of the variables only randomly being the values of 0 or 1. As a consequence, we present an *adaptive* DPLL (i.e., Davis-Putnam-Logemann-Loveland) (ADPLL for short) algorithm to deal with our probability computation problem. ADPLL recursively selects the most frequent variable in a condition ϕ, and breaks the conjuncts's dependence in the condition as quickly as possible, thereby speeding up the probability computation.

Algorithm 4.9 shows the pseudo-code of ADPLL algorithm. It takes as inputs a condition ϕ of an object and an initial probability *prob*, and outputs the probability of the condition, i.e.,

[8]Available at https://en.wikipedia.org/wiki/Sharp-SAT.

Algorithm 4.9 Adaptive DPLL Search (ADPLL)

Input: a condition ϕ, a probability *prob* (*prob* = 1 when invoked firstly)
Output: the probability of the condition $\Pr(\phi)$

1: $\Pr(\phi) \longleftarrow 0$
2: **if** the conjuncts in ϕ are independent $\|$ ϕ = *true* or *false* **then**
3:      compute the probability of ϕ, i.e., $\Pr(\phi)$
4:      **return** prob$\cdot \Pr(\phi)$
5: **end if**
6: select a variable v that appears the most times in ϕ
7: **for all** assignment v_a of v **do**
8:      $\phi' \longleftarrow \phi(v = v_a)$
9:      $\Pr(\phi) \longleftarrow \Pr(\phi)+$ ADPLL$(\phi', prob\cdot p(v_a))$
10: **end for**
11: **return** $\Pr(\phi)$

$\Pr(\phi)$. It is important to note that the parameter *prob* is initialized as one when other functions invoke ADPLL algorithm. Specifically, ADPLL initializes the probability $\Pr(\phi)$ to zero (line 1). If ϕ is *true* (or *false*), ADPLL returns $\Pr(\phi)$ as 1 (or 0). If the conjuncts in ϕ are independent (i.e., each conjunct in ϕ has different variables), ADPLL directly computes and returns $\Pr(\phi)$ via leveraging the special conjunctive rule and the general disjunctive rule (lines 2–5). To be more specific, the special conjunctive rule claims that, for two conjuncts p and q, if they are independent, the probability $\Pr(p \wedge q) = \Pr(p) \cdot \Pr(q)$. In addition, the general disjunctive rule is, for any two disjuncts p and q, the probability $\Pr(p \vee q) = 1 - \Pr(\neg p \wedge \neg q)$, which is employed to derive the probability of each conjunct in the condition (where several disjuncts are contained in the conjunct).

Otherwise, when the conjuncts in the condition ϕ are dependent, ADPLL selects a variable v if it occurs the most times in ϕ. A random selection breaks the tier if the occurrence times of the variables are identical (line 6). In the sequel, for each possible value v_a of the variable v, ADPLL first gets a new condition ϕ' by substituting v_a for the variable v in ϕ (line 8). Then, it updates $\Pr(\phi)$ by adding the value of probability returned by ADPLL$(\phi', prob \cdot p(v_a))$ (line 9). Here, $p(v_a)$ denotes the probability of variable v getting the value v_a under the learned data distribution in the preprocessing step. At this time, ADPLL is recursively invoked with the inputs of new updated ϕ' and updated probability $prob \cdot p(v_a)$. It is worth noting that when the probability $\Pr(\phi)$ can be calculated directly (i.e., ϕ = *true* or *false*, or the conjuncts in ϕ are independent), ADPLL returns $\Pr(\phi)$ at line 4 of Algorithm 4.9. Then, it returns to line 9 of Algorithm 4.9 of the previous layer ADPLL recall (if exists) and continues processing the "foreach" loop of this ADPLL.

Example 4.23   Take the condition of o_5, i.e., $\phi(o_5)$, shown in Table 4.2, as an example. For the sake of simplicity, assume that the probability distribution of each attribute is as follows. The probability of attribute a_2 getting the value i, i.e., $p(a_2 = i)$, is 0.1, $i = 0, 1, \cdots, 9$. Similarly, the probability $p(a_3 = i) = 0.125$, $i = 0, 1, \cdots, 7$. The probability $p(a_4 = i) = 0.1$, $i = 0, 1, 5$; $p(a_4 = i) = 0.2$, $i = 2, 3$; and $p(a_4 = 4) = 0.3$. The parameter of $prob$ in ADPLL is initialized to one.

First of all, since the three variables $Var(o_5, a_2)$, $Var(o_5, a_3)$, and $Var(o_5, a_4)$ occur two times in $\phi(o_5)$ (as depicted in Table 4.2), ADPLL randomly selects one of the three variables, e.g., the variable $Var(o_5, a_4)$. Then, ADPLL assigns one possible value to it, e.g., $Var(o_5, a_4) = 0$. Note that, according to the probability distribution of the attribute a_4, the probability of getting the value 0, i.e., $p(Var(o_5, a_4) = 0)$, is 0.1. As a result, when the value of 0 substitutes for $Var(o_5, a_4)$ in the condition $\phi(o_5)$, $\phi'(o_5)$ becomes $[(Var(o_5, a_2) > 2) \vee (Var(o_5, a_3) > 3)] \wedge [(Var(o_5, a_2) > Var(o_2, a_2)) \vee (Var(o_5, a_3) > 2)]$. Taking the condition $\phi'(o_5)$ and $prob \cdot p(Var(o_5, a_4) = 0)$ (= 0.1) as inputs, another ADPLL search is invoked.

In the second-layer of ADPLL search, assume that $Var(o_5, a_3)$ is selected and is assigned the value of 0. Based on the supposed probability distribution of a_3, $p(Var(o_5, a_3) = 0) = 0.125$. At this time, $\phi''(o_5) = (Var(o_5, a_2) > 2) \wedge (Var(o_5, a_2) > Var(o_2, a_2))$, after the value of 0 substitutes for the $Var(o_5, a_3)$ in the condition ϕ'. Another new ADPLL search is recalled with the parameters $\phi''(o_5)$ and the probability (0.1×0.125). When entering the third-layer of ADPLL search, assume that $Var(o_5, a_2)$ is chosen and is assigned the value of 0, where $p(Var(o_5, a_2) = 0) = 0.1$. At this time, $\phi'''(o_5)$ = false. One more new ADPLL search is recalled with the parameters $\phi'''(o_5)$ and the probability $(0.1 \times 0.125 \times 0.1)$.

For the fourth-layer of ADPLL search, as $\phi'''(o_5)$ = false, it executes lines 2–4 of Algorithm 4.9. It gets and returns $\Pr(\phi'''(o_5)) = 0$. Then, it comes back to the third layer of ADPLL search (i.e., line 8 of Algorithm 4.9); the probability $\Pr(\phi''(o_5))$ is still zero. In a similar way, it finishes the "foreach" loop of the third layer of ADPLL search after setting $Var(o_5, a_2)$ as values from 1 to 9 one by one. Next, it returns to the "foreach" loop of the second layer of ADPLL search, and sets $Var(o_5, a_3)$ as values from 1 to 7 one by one. Thereafter, it returns to the "foreach" loop of the first layer of ADPLL search. After assigning $Var(o_5, a_4)$ as values from 1 to 5 one by one, the probability $\Pr(\phi(o_5)) = 0.823$ is obtained.

In addition, for ease of further understanding the general procedure of ADPLL search for computing $\Pr(\phi(o_5))$, we partition the whole variable value space into several blocks, as illustrated in Table 4.4, where each variable changes its value monotonically from the smallest to the biggest. Note that we aggregate the adjacent variable value combinations (i.e., assignments) together as a block if all in the block make the condition to get the same value of $true$ (or $false$). In total, all the assignments are permutated into 22 blocks, as shown in Table 4.4. The table also gives the corresponding probability for each block, i.e., the probability of the assignments w.r.t. the block making the condition get the value of $true$. In particular, the word "Any" in Table 4.4 corresponding to a certain variable means that the variable gets all its possible values.

In fact, the probability of each block i can be derived directly by $p(Var(o_5, a_4)) \cdot p(Var(o_5, a_3)) \cdot p(Var(o_5, a_2)) \cdot p(Var(o_2, a_2))$, in which $p(Var(o_x, a_y))$ is equal to the probabil-

Table 4.4: Example of ADPLL algorithm

Block	Var (o_5, a_4)	Var (o_5, a_3)	Var (o_5, a_2)	Var (o_2, a_2)	Probability
1	0-2	0-2	0-2	Any	0 (False)
2	0-2	0-2	3	0-2	0.0045
3	0-2	0-2	3	3-9	0 (False)
4	0-2	0-2	4	0-3	0.006
5	0-2	0-2	4	4-9	0 (False)
6	0-2	0-2	5	0-4	0.0075
7	0-2	0-2	5	5-9	0 (False)
8	0-2	0-2	6	0-5	0.009
9	0-2	0-2	6	6-9	0 (False)
10	0-2	0-2	7	0-6	0.0105
11	0-2	0-2	7	7-9	0 (False)
12	0-2	0-2	8	0-7	0.0120
13	0-2	0-2	8	8-9	0 (False)
14	0-2	0-2	9	0-8	0.0135
15	0-2	0-2	9	9	0 (False)
16	0-2	3	0-2	Any	0 (False)
17	0-2	3	3-9	Any	0.035
18	0-2	4-7	Any	Any	0-2
19	3-4	0-3	0-2	Any	0 (False)
20	3-4	0-3	3-9	Any	0.175
21	3-4	4-7	Any	Any	0.25
22	5	Any	Any	Any	0.1

ity of $Var(o_x, a_y)$ getting the corresponding values in block i. Finally, the probability $\Pr(\phi(o_5))$ is the accumulated probability over the 22 blocks. Note that, in Table 4.4, there are 10 blocks with the probability zero. This is because the corresponding assignments of those 10 blocks make the condition get the value of *false*, as highlighted in the last column of Table 4.4.

It is easily known that the probability computation for each condition is of complexity $O(N^V)$ if N is the average number of the possible values that one variable could get, and V denotes the average number of variables that each condition consists of. As mentioned earlier, the problem of probability computation is at least as hard as the weighted model counting problem (i.e., #SAT problem). What is exciting is that ADPLL is an efficient heuristic algorithm that could get the accurate probability of the condition quickly. It results from the relatively less correlated variables in the conditions. In addition, it is worthwhile to mention that approximate probability computation [Fink et al., 2013] is a promising direction for the problem.

4.3.4 CROWD TASK SELECTION

Paying crowd workers to check all the expressions in the conditions is prohibitively expensive, and thus, we must be judicious with which expressions are selected for crowdsourcing preferentially. In this part, we introduce the utility function of selecting a task to crowdsource, and present a novel algorithm to facilitate BayesCrowd.

The Utility Function

Intuitively, if the probability $\Pr(\phi(o))$ is skewed toward 0 or 1, we expect to predict whether the object o is a query result object with reasonable accuracy. On the other hand, if $\Pr(\phi(o))$ is a fair coin flip, we have no reliable information about whether o is a query result object.

It is natural to use Shannon entropy as a metric to quantify the quality of the query result set. Specifically, we define the entropy of an object in terms of its confidence $\Pr(\phi(o))$ (denoted as p_o for short) by Eq. (4.18).

$$H(o) = -\left(p_o \cdot \log_2 p_o + (1 - p_o) \cdot \log_2 (1 - p_o)\right). \qquad (4.18)$$

In order to prioritize the tasks and crowdsource the most beneficial ones preferentially, we introduce the expected marginal utility function to measure the benefit of crowdsourcing the tasks for answering the queries. The function is defined as the *information gain* based on the entropy function, as stated in Definition 4.24.

Definition 4.24 (**The marginal utility function**). Given an incomplete dataset $\mathcal{O}$ and a query Q, for the condition $\phi(o)$ of an object $o \in \mathcal{O}$, the (expected) marginal utility function, denoted as $\mathcal{G}$, of selecting an expression e (i.e., the task) to crowdsource is defined in Eq. (4.19).

$$\mathcal{G}(o, e) = H(o) - \mathbb{E}[H(o|e)] \qquad (4.19)$$

$$\mathbb{E}[H(o|e)] = \Pr(e) \cdot H(o|e = \text{true}) + (1 - \Pr(e)) \cdot H(o|e = \text{false}). \qquad (4.20)$$

Here, $\Pr(e)$ represents the probability of the expression e obtaining a true value. $H(o|e = \text{true/false})$ denotes the entropy of the object o after the expression e in its condition gets the value of *true/false*.

In fact, the function $\mathcal{G}(o, e)$ is defined as the expected quality improvement for the object o when crowdsourcing the expression e in the condition $\phi(o)$.

We would like to explain that crowdsourcing work faces budget constraints in most cases, since posting all the tasks is prohibitively expensive. Thus, we should spend no more than the budget constraint (e.g., B) on maximizing the expected marginal utility as much as we can.

Without loss of generality, the budget B is regarded as the number of the tasks that the requester could crowdsource (assuming that crowdsourcing a task needs a fixed monetary cost).

On the other hand, in many situations, the latency is a key factor that the requester is usually concerned about. For instance, let's say the requester would like to finish the task within five time units. Thus, here we borrow the idea from [Das Sarma et al., 2014, Fan et al., 2015] that the latency is measured by the number of iterations in the crowd query. Specifically, the tasks posted in one iteration are thought to be completed almost at the same time. Hence, adjusting the number of tasks in one iteration could control the latency of the crowd query (if the total number of tasks is fixed).

Task Selection Algorithm

We propose a novel task selection algorithm for implementing the second phase of BayesCrowd. It takes into account budget constraints while allowing us to control the latency.

Algorithm 4.10 depicts the pseudo-code of task selection algorithm. It takes as inputs an incomplete dataset $\mathcal{O}$, a query Q with the c-table $\mathcal{C}$, a budget constraint B, and a latency requirement L, and outputs the set of selected crowd tasks, denoted as $\mathcal{T}$. First of all, the algorithm empties the result set $\mathcal{R}$, and estimates the number of tasks in one batch/iteration, denoted by μ, via computing $\lceil \frac{B}{L} \rceil$ (line 1). Then, the task selection algorithm starts to choose the tasks to crowdsource (lines 2–21). Specifically, it recalls the function ADPLL to select a group of objects with the size $\min(B, \mu)$ that have the highest entropies. The selected objects are collected in the set $\mathcal{O}_t$. Meanwhile, the budget B is updated (lines 4–9). In the following, for each object $o \in \mathcal{O}_t$, the task selection algorithm chooses the expression $e^\star$ from $\phi(o)$ that has the largest expected utility improvement. Next, the expression $e^\star$ is added to the set $\mathcal{T}$, which is employed to collect the awaiting crowd tasks in this iteration (lines 10–20). Finally, the algorithms returns the selected task set $\mathcal{T}$ and stops (line 22).

Algorithm 4.10 has shown how to obtain the task set $\mathcal{T}$ for crowdsourcing. Here we would like to mention that BayesCrowd allows us to post/push the awaiting crowd tasks in batches. In other words, during each batch/iteration, BayesCrowd recalls the task selection algorithm (i.e., Algorithm 4.10) to get the task set $\mathcal{T}$ within the constraints of budget and latency. This batch-style task crowdsourcing mechanism provides an opportunity for BayesCrowd to take into account the new returned task answers during task selection in the next iteration. Thus, the next batch of awaiting crowd tasks is chosen optimally, i.e., selecting the most beneficial tasks to the requester's utility according to all the received answers.

In addition, it is important to note that since conflicting tasks may lead to unreasonable results, a batch of tasks in one iteration must not conflict. In our implementation, we tackle the conflicts via identifying the variables in the chosen tasks (i.e., expressions) and make sure that any two of the chosen tasks in one iteration do not share the same variable.

Algorithm 4.10 Task Selection Algorithm

Input: an incomplete dataset $\mathcal{O}$; a query Q with c-table $\mathcal{C}$; a budget constraint B, a latency requirement L

Output: the selected task set $\mathcal{T}$ for crowdsourcing

1:   $\mathcal{R} \longleftarrow \varnothing; \mu \longleftarrow \lceil \frac{B}{L} \rceil$
2:   **if** the budget $B \neq 0$ and there is an expression in conditions **then**
3:     $\mathcal{T} \longleftarrow \mathcal{O}_t \longleftarrow \varnothing$
4:     **for all** object $o \in \mathcal{O}$ **do**
5:       $p_o \longleftarrow \mathsf{ADPLL}(\phi(o), 1)$
6:       $H(o) \longleftarrow -p_o \cdot \log_2 p_o - (1 - p_o) \cdot \log_2(1 - p_o)$ // Eq. (4.18)
7:     **end for**
8:     add $\min(B, \mu)$ objects o having the highest $H(o)$ to $\mathcal{O}_t$
9:     $B \longleftarrow \max(B - \mu, 0)$
10:     **for all** object $o \in \mathcal{O}_t$ **do**
11:       $g \longleftarrow 0$
12:       **for all** expression $e \in \phi(o)$ **do**
13:         $\mathbb{E}[H(o|e)] \longleftarrow \Pr(e) \cdot H(o|e = \text{true}) + (1 - \Pr(e)) \cdot H(o|e = \text{false})$ // Eq. (4.20)
14:         $\mathcal{G}(o, e) \longleftarrow H(o) - \mathbb{E}[H(o|e)]$ // Eq. (4.19)
15:         **if** $\mathcal{G}(o, e) > g$ **then**
16:           $g \longleftarrow \mathcal{G}(o, e); e^\star \longleftarrow e$
17:         **end if**
18:       **end for**
19:       $\mathcal{T} \longleftarrow \mathcal{T} + \{e^\star\}$
20:     **end for**
21:   **end if**
22:   **return** $\mathcal{T}$

Example 4.25   Take the skyline query on the sample data as an example. For sake of simplicity, it is assumed that the budget $B = 6$ and the latency requirement $L = 3$, indicating two tasks are posted on the crowdsourcing market in each iteration.

First, considering the condition of each object shown in Table 4.2, the task selection algorithm computes the entropy of each object. The conditions of o_2 and o_3 have gotten a true value (i.e., the entropy is zero). As a result, the result set $\mathcal{R} = \{o_2, o_3\}$. Then, it derives the entropies of the other three objects as follows. The entropy of o_1, i.e., $H(o_1) = 0.72$. The entropy $H(o_4) = 0.62$, and the entropy $H(o_5) = 0.67$. Hence, it chooses the objects o_1 and o_5 (that have the highest entropies) to form the set $\mathcal{O}_t$. Next, for each of the two objects, the task selection algorithm selects one task from its condition. Specifically, for the object o_1, its condition $\phi(o_1) = (Var(o_5, a_2) < 2) \vee (Var(o_5, a_3) < 3) \vee (Var(o_5, a_4) < 4)$. There are three expressions (denoted as e_1, e_2, and e_3) in the condition $\phi(o_1)$, namely, $e_1 = \text{Var}(o_5, a_2) < 2$, $e_2 = \text{Var}(o_5, a_3) < 3$, and $e_3 = \text{Var}(o_5, a_4) < 4$. Then, it derives the individual marginal utility of each expression, i.e., $\mathcal{G}(o_1, e_1) = 0.072$, $\mathcal{G}(o_1, e_2) = 0.157$, and $\mathcal{G}(o_1, e_3) = 0.322$. Hence, the expression e_3 is chosen to crowdsource. Similarly, for the condition $\phi(o_5)$, the expression $\text{Var}(o_5, a_3) > 3$ is selected. Thereafter, the two tasks are posted on the crowdsourcing market by our framework BayesCrowd.

Assume that the returned answers are $\text{Var}(o_5, a_4) < 4$ and $\text{Var}(o_5, a_3) = 3$. Using these results, the original c-table (shown in Table 4.2) is updated as a new c-table, as depicted in Table 4.5. The result set $\mathcal{R}$ is updated as $\{o_1, o_2, o_3\}$. In the following, BayesCrowd enters the second iteration of task selection. It invokes the task selection algorithm, and gets $\mathcal{O}_t = \{o_5, o_4\}$ due to $H(o_4) = 0.63$ and $H(o_5) = 0.88$. Similarly, BayesCrowd chooses the expressions $\text{Var}(o_5, a_2) > 2$ and $\text{Var}(o_2, a_2) < 3$ from the conditions of the two objects, respectively, which are posted on the crowdsourcing platform. Assume that the returned answers are $\text{Var}(o_5, a_2) > 2$ and $\text{Var}(o_2, a_2) > 3$. Thus, $\phi(o_4) = \text{false}$, and $\phi(o_5) = \text{true}$. The result set $\mathcal{R}$ becomes $\{o_1, o_2, o_3, o_5\}$. So far, none of the conditions has an expression. Therefore, BayesCrowd returns the result set $\mathcal{R}$ and terminates.

Table 4.5: The updated c-table with budget $B = 6$ and latency requirement $L = 3$

Object	Condition
o_1	True
o_2	True
o_3	True
o_4	$(\text{Var}(o_2; a_2) < 3) \wedge [(\text{Var}(o_5; a_2) < 3) \vee (\text{Var}(o_5; a_4) < 2)]$
o_5	$\text{Var}(o_5; a_2) > 2$

Discussion

Utility-cost analysis. Based on the marginal utility function in Definition 4.24, we can calculate the total utility that the requester obtains from BayesCrowd. Specifically, if there is no expression in the conditions of the c-table when the query finishes (i.e., all the entropies are zero), the total utility, denoted by $\kappa(Q)$, is written as Eq. (4.21).

$$\kappa(Q) = \sum_{o \in \mathcal{O}} H(o). \tag{4.21}$$

In particular, $H(o)$ is defined in Eq. (4.18). It is the entropy of an object o in terms of its initial probability of o being a result object. Note that, the initial probability is derived based on the original condition of o before BayesCrowd enters the crowdsourcing phase.

Let E (V) be the average number of expressions (variables) in a condition, N be the number of possible values that a variable can have. For a given budget constraint B and a latency constraint L, the computation cost of BayesCrowd, denoted as $cost_c$, can be written by Eq. (4.22).

$$cost_c = L \cdot \left(|\mathcal{O}| \cdot N^V + \left\lceil \frac{B}{L} \right\rceil \cdot E + |\mathcal{O}| \right).$$
(4.22)

Note that the computation cost mainly consists of the cost of the object selection (via computing the entropy), the expression (task) selection, and the c-table update after each iteration of task selection.

In addition, the monetary cost of BayesCrowd, denoted as $cost_m$, can be written by Eq. (4.23), where d is the number of attributes, $|\mathcal{D}|$ is the average number of the objects in dominator sets, N_w is the number of workers we employ for each task, and r_0 is the base reward for each answer.

$$cost_m = |\mathcal{O}| \cdot |\mathcal{D}| \cdot d \cdot N_w \cdot r_0.$$
(4.23)

In particular, each task is assigned to N_w workers, and there are at most $|\mathcal{O}| \cdot |\mathcal{D}| \cdot d$ expressions. Note that when it comes to the case of budget constraint, $cost_m$ should be not larger than the budget.

Quality control. The quality of the result set (w.r.t. the requester's utility in this book) can be improved from two aspects. We have carefully explained how to boost query quality through selecting the tasks wisely. Another way of improving quality is to incentivize workers to return high-quality answers. One promising strategy is to offer a bonus for the workers if they do a good job, in addition to paying a base reward. Nonetheless, in some cases, some workers always answer the task correctly even without the bonus, while others return incorrect answers even with the bonus. Consequently, how to incentivize workers wisely is another key aspect to further boost query quality, which is also our focus in the future work.

CHAPTER 5

Conclusions

Due to the universality of data incompleteness, answering queries on incomplete data has received much attention from researchers. As a result, query processing over incomplete databases has become an increasingly important, yet challenging, research topic. Although there are many previous studies on efficient query processing for traditional complete data, the intrinsic characteristics of complete data prevent their direct application to the incomplete data case.

In this book, we discuss various aspects of query processing over incomplete databases, including indexing structures, diverse query types, and existing management systems of incomplete data. In particular, after briefly introducing the incomplete data handling methods, the book focuses on three types of representative queries in the context of incomplete data, viz., k-nearest neighbor search, skyline query, and top-k dominating query. Starting from the key challenges and the intrinsic characteristics of the corresponding query, the book presents some advanced query processing techniques, which consist of effective indexing, pruning, and crowd-sourcing techniques, for answering these queries over incomplete data.

Chapter 1 describes the typical and useful indexes for supporting incomplete data, including the bitstring-augmented index, MOSAIC, bitmap, and VA file. The bitstring-augmented index helps to avoid skewing the data by assigning missing values to several distinct values, while it is infeasible for high dimensions. In contrast, MOSAIC is better than the bitstring-augmented index for point queries, but it is not useful for multiple-dimension range queries. Bitmap is able to achieve high search efficiency at the cost of large storage consumption. However, compared with bitmap, VA file has lower search efficiency for relatively smaller storage consumption. In addition, the chapter surveys efforts on queries over incomplete data, including similarity search and skyline query on incomplete data, incomplete data stream queries, etc. Also, it summarizes the existing management systems on incomplete data.

Chapter 2 explores the incompleteness handling methods, which can be categorized into three categories: the data discarding model, which is to simply remove the objects with missing values and operate only on the complete objects; the data imputation model, which replaces the missing data with the imputed values; and the observed-data dependent model, which does not discard any object that has missing attribute value(s) and deals with the incomplete data using new designated models and definitions such as the typical representation system. In particular, a variety of imputation methods are further studied, including statistical imputation (e.g., mean/mode imputation and multiple imputation), machine learning-based imputation (e.g.,

Naive Bayes), and some modern imputation methods (e.g., using computational intelligence, crowdsourcing, web information, rules, etc.).

Chapter 3 introduces three representative queries over incomplete data from the two aspects of background and definitions. For k-nearest neighbor search, skyline query, and top-k dominating query, this chapter describes the query definitions in the context of both complete and incomplete databases, with illustrative examples and related work on complete data.

Chapter 4 elaborates some advanced query processing techniques for k-nearest neighbor search, skyline query, and top-k dominating query over incomplete data. This chapter first presents several novel index structures, such as LαB index, histogram index, and bitmap index. On top of these index structures, it then introduces a suite of effective pruning heuristics for these three queries, which contain α value pruning, histogram-based pruning, skyband pruning, upper bound score pruning, etc. Last but not least, the chapter explains the problem of how to leverage crowdsourcing techniques to solve skyline query over incomplete data with high accuracy but affordable cost.

It is worth mentioning that there are a number of relevant issues that this book has not covered or has covered briefly. Incomplete data mining is one important topic which is not included. Another issue is data integration and cleaning struggles with incomplete data. Also, we only discuss the data imputation issues briefly.

Last but not least, there are many open problems in this area.

- New incomplete data indexes. Although there are a few indexes supporting incomplete data, they may not be powerful for a variety of queries on incomplete data. Thus, it is very useful to design new efficient index structures for incomplete data. As an example, indexing missing data via metric space techniques could be a promising direction.

- New queries over incomplete data. With the rapid development of information technologies and web applications, it appears there are a number of new and complicated demands (w.r.t. new queries). Hence, efficient and effective techniques and algorithms are desirable for those queries.

- Using crowdsourcing to optimize incomplete data management. In many applications, the computers may not work well, since it is rather hard for machines to learn useful information on missing values. But, human intelligence is good at learning this kind of information. There are a few researchers working on the problem of incomplete data with the support of crowdsourcing, and hence, there is much room for crowdsourcing to improve the management of incomplete data.

- Exploratory search in incomplete databases. It is very likely for the query result on incomplete data to be dissatisfying. Providing new exploratory functionality that helps users to find what they are looking for (via interactively and repeatedly consulting the user to manage query conditions [Qarabaqi and Riedewald, 2014]) might facilitate the improvement of query quality.

- Generic incomplete data management systems. There is no general incomplete data management system that incorporates the incomplete data models as well as supporting queries and explanations over incomplete data. If one could deploy such a system, it would benefit many applications suffering from incomplete data.

Bibliography

S. Abiteboul, P. Kanellakis, and G. Grahne. On the representation and querying of sets of possible worlds. *Theoretical Computer Science*, 78(1):159–187, 1991. DOI: 10.1016/0304-3975(51)90007-2 3

S. Abiteboul, R. Hull, and V. Vianu. *Foundations of Databases*. Addison-Wesley Longman Publishing Co., Inc., 1995. 3

P. H. Abreu, H. Amaro, D. C. Silva, P. Machado, M. H. Abreu, N. Afonso, and A. Dourado. Overall survival prediction for women breast cancer using ensemble methods and incomplete clinical data. In *13th Mediterranean Conference on Medical and Biological Engineering and Computing*, pages 1366–1369, Springer, 2014. DOI: 10.1007/978-3-319-00846-2_338 3

A. A. Alwan, H. Ibrahim, N. I. Udzir, and F. Sidi. Processing skyline queries in incomplete distributed databases. *Journal of Intelligent Information Systems*, 48(2):399–420, 2017. DOI: 10.1007/s10844-016-0419-2 9

L. Antova, C. Koch, and D. Olteanu. MayBMS: Managing incomplete information with probabilistic world-set decompositions. In *ICDE*, pages 1479–1480, IEEE, 2007. DOI: 10.1109/icde.2007.369042 12

M. T. Asif, N. Mitrovic, L. Garg, J. Dauwels, and P. Jaillet. Low-dimensional models for missing data imputation in road networks. In *ICASSP*, pages 3527–3531, IEEE, 2013. DOI: 10.1109/icassp.2013.6638314 23

M. Aste, M. Boninsegna, A. Freno, and E. Trentin. Techniques for dealing with incomplete data: A tutorial and survey. *Pattern Analysis and Applications*, 18(1):1–29, 2015. DOI: 10.1007/s10044-014-0411-9 23

M. J. Atallah, Y. Qi, and H. Yuan. Asymptotically efficient algorithms for skyline probabilities of uncertain data. *ACM Transactions on Database Systems*, 36(2):12, 2011. DOI: 10.1145/1966385.1966390 29

I. B. Aydilek and A. Arslan. A hybrid method for imputation of missing values using optimized fuzzy c-means with support vector regression and a genetic algorithm. *Information Sciences*, 233:25–35, 2013. DOI: 10.1016/j.ins.2013.01.021 23

G. Babanejad, H. Ibrahim, N. I. Udzir, F. Sidi, and A. A. A. Aljuboori. Finding skyline points over dynamic incomplete database. In *Malaysian National Conference on Databases*, 2014. DOI: 10.13140/2.1.1270.8162. 9

I. Bartolini, P. Ciaccia, and M. Patella. Efficient sort-based skyline evaluation. *ACM Transactions on Database Systems*, 33(4):31, 2008. DOI: 10.1145/1412331.1412343 29

N. Beckmann, H.-P. Kriegel, R. Schneider, and B. Seeger. The R*-tree: An efficient and robust access method for points and rectangles. In *SIGMOD*, pages 322–331, ACM, 1990. DOI: 10.1145/93605.98741 29

T. Bernecker, T. Emrich, H.-P. Kriegel, N. Mamoulis, M. Renz, and A. Züfle. A novel probabilistic pruning approach to speed up similarity queries in uncertain databases. In *ICDE*, pages 339–350, IEEE, 2011. DOI: 10.1109/icde.2011.5767908 26, 27

R. Bharuka and P. S. Kumar. Finding skylines for incomplete data. In *ADC*, pages 109–117, 2013a. 8

R. Bharuka and P. S. Kumar. Finding superior skyline points from incomplete data. In *Proc. of International Conference on Management of Data*, pages 35–44, Computer Society of India, 2013b. 9

S. Borzsonyi, D. Kossmann, and K. Stocker. The skyline operator. In *ICDE*, pages 421–430, 2001. DOI: 10.1109/icde.2001.914855 28, 29

S. Brinis, A. J. Traina, and C. Traina Jr. Analyzing missing data in metric spaces. *Journal of Information and Data Management*, 5(3):224, 2014. 1, 6, 17

G. Canahuate, M. Gibas, and H. Ferhatosmanoglu. Indexing incomplete databases. In *EDBT*, pages 884–901, Springer, 2006. DOI: 10.1007/11687238_52 4, 5

C.-Y. Chan, H. V. Jagadish, K.-L. Tan, A. K. Tung, and Z. Zhang. Finding k-dominant skylines in high dimensional space. In *SIGMOD*, pages 503–514, ACM, 2006. DOI: 10.1145/1142473.1142530 30

J. R. Cheema. A review of missing data handling methods in education research. *Review of Educational Research*, 84(4):487–508, 2014. DOI: 10.3102/0034654314532697 23

L. Chen and X. Lian. Query processing over uncertain databases. *Synthesis Lectures on Data Management*, 4(6):1–101, 2012. DOI: 10.2200/s00465ed1v01y201212dtm033 4

R. Cheng, D. V. Kalashnikov, and S. Prabhakar. Evaluating probabilistic queries over imprecise data. In *SIGMOD*, pages 551–562, ACM, 2003. DOI: 10.1145/872819.872823 26

R. Cheng, D. V. Kalashnikov, and S. Prabhakar. Querying imprecise data in moving object environments. *IEEE Transactions on Knowledge Data Engineering*, 16(9):1112–1127, 2004. DOI: 10.1109/tkde.2004.46 26

R. Cheng, J. Chen, M. Mokbel, and C.-Y. Chow. Probabilistic verifiers: Evaluating constrained nearest-neighbor queries over uncertain data. In *ICDE*, pages 973–982, IEEE, 2008. DOI: 10.1109/icde.2008.4497506 26

R. Cheng, L. Chen, J. Chen, and X. Xie. Evaluating probability threshold k-nearest-neighbor queries over uncertain data. In *EDBT/ICDT*, pages 672–683, ACM, 2009a. DOI: 10.1145/1516360.1516438 26

W. Cheng, X. Jin, and J.-T. Sun. Probabilistic similarity query on dimension incomplete data. In *ICDM*, pages 81–90, IEEE, 2009b. DOI: 10.1109/icdm.2009.72 7, 14

W. Cheng, X. Jin, J.-T. Sun, X. Lin, X. Zhang, and W. Wang. Searching dimension incomplete databases. *IEEE Transactions on Knowledge Data Engineering*, 26(3):725–738, 2014. DOI: 10.1109/tkde.2013.14 7, 14, 17, 66

K. L. Cheung and A. W.-C. Fu. Enhanced nearest neighbor search on the R-tree. *ACM SIGMOD Record*, 27(3):16–21, 1998. DOI: 10.1145/290593.290596 26

J. Chomicki, P. Godfrey, J. Gryz, and D. Liang. Skyline with presorting. In *ICDE*, pages 717–719, 2003. DOI: 10.1109/icde.2003.1260846 29

X. Chu, J. Morcos, I. F. Ilyas, M. Ouzzani, P. Papotti, N. Tang, and Y. Ye. KATARA: A data cleaning system powered by knowledge bases and crowdsourcing. In *SIGMOD*, pages 1247–1261, ACM, 2015. DOI: 10.1145/2723372.2749431 22

E. Ciceri, P. Fraternali, D. Martinenghi, and M. Tagliasacchi. Crowdsourcing for top-k query processing over uncertain data. *IEEE Transactions on Knowledge Data Engineering*, 28(1): 41–53, 2016. DOI: 10.1109/icde.2016.7498370 12

F. Cismondi, A. S. Fialho, S. M. Vieira, S. R. Reti, J. M. Sousa, and S. N. Finkelstein. Missing data in medical databases: Impute, delete or classify? *Artificial Intelligence in Medicine*, 58(1): 63–72, 2013. DOI: 10.1016/j.artmed.2013.01.003 23

A. Colantonio and R. Di Pietro. CONCISE: Compressed "n" composable integer set. *Information Processing Letters*, 110(16):644–650, 2010a. DOI: 10.1016/j.ipl.2010.05.018 43, 71

D. Comer. Ubiquitous b-tree. *ACM Computing Surveys (CSUR)*, 11(2):121–137, 1979. DOI: 10.1145/356770.356776 39

A. Cuzzocrea and A. Nucita. I-SQE: A query engine for answering range queries over incomplete spatial databases. In *KES*, pages 91–101, Springer, 2009a. DOI: 10.1007/978-3-642-04592-9_12 8

A. Cuzzocrea and A. Nucita. Reasoning on incompleteness of spatial information for effectively and efficiently answering range queries over incomplete spatial databases. In *FQAS*, pages 37–52, Springer, 2009b. DOI: 10.1007/978-3-642-04957-6_4 8

A. Cuzzocrea and A. Nucita. Enhancing accuracy and expressive power of range query answers over incomplete spatial databases via a novel reasoning approach. *Data and Knowledge Engineering*, 70(8):702–716, 2011. DOI: 10.1016/j.datak.2011.03.002 66

S. Dan, O. Dan, R. Christopher, and K. Christoph. Probabilistic databases. *Synthesis Lectures on Data Management*, 3(2):1–180, 2011. DOI: 10.2200/s00362ed1v01y201105dtm016 4

A. Das Sarma, A. Parameswaran, H. Garcia-Molina, and A. Halevy. Crowd-powered find algorithms. In *ICDE*, pages 964–975, IEEE, 2014. DOI: 10.1109/icde.2014.6816715 78

S. B. Davidson, S. Khanna, T. Milo, and S. Roy. Using the crowd for top-*k* and group-by queries. In *ICDT*, pages 225–236, ACM, 2013. DOI: 10.1145/2448496.2448524 12

L. de Alfaro, V. Polychronopoulos, and N. Polyzotis. Efficient techniques for crowdsourced top-*k* lists. In *4th AAAI Conference on Human Computation and Crowdsourcing*, 2016. DOI: 10.24963/ijcai.2017/670 12

H. de Jong and D. Ropers. Strategies for dealing with incomplete information in the modeling of molecular interaction networks. *Briefings in Bioinformatics*, 7(4):354–363, 2006. DOI: 10.1093/bib/bbl034 2

Y. Deville, D. Gilbert, J. Van Helden, and S. J. Wodak. An overview of data models for the analysis of biochemical pathways. *Briefings in Bioinformatics*, 4(3):246–259, 2003. DOI: 10.1007/3-540-36481-1_23 2

J. K. Dixon. Pattern recognition with partly missing data. *IEEE Transactions on Systems, Man, and Cybernetics*, 9(10):617–621, 1979. DOI: 10.1109/tsmc.1979.4310090 27

H. Elmeleegy, J. Madhavan, and A. Halevy. Harvesting relational tables from lists on the Web. *PVLDB*, 2(1):1078–1089, 2009. DOI: 10.1007/s00778-011-0223-0 22

C. K. Enders. Dealing with missing data in developmental research. *Child Development Perspectives*, 7(1):27–31, 2013. DOI: 10.1111/cdep.12008 23

J. Fan, M. Zhang, S. Kok, M. Lu, and B. C. Ooi. Crowdop: Query optimization for declarative crowdsourcing systems. *IEEE Transactions on Knowledge and Data Engineering*, 27(8):2078–2092, 2015. DOI: 10.1109/icde.2016.7498417 78

W. Fan. Dependencies revisited for improving data quality. In *SIGMOD*, pages 159–170, ACM, 2008. DOI: 10.1145/1376916.1376940 22

W. Fan, J. Li, S. Ma, N. Tang, and W. Yu. Towards certain fixes with editing rules and master data. *PVLDB*, 3(1-2):173–184, 2010. DOI: 10.1007/s00778-011-0253-7 22

A. Farhangfar, L. Kurgan, W. Pedrycz, et al. A novel framework for imputation of missing values in databases. *IEEE Transactions on Systems, Man, and Cybernetics*, 37(5):692–709, 2007. DOI: 10.1109/tsmca.2007.902631 20

E. Fernández-Vázquez. Recovering matrices of economic flows from incomplete data and a composite prior. *Entropy*, 12(3):516–527, 2010. DOI: 10.3390/e12030516 2

F. Fessant and S. Midenet. Self-organising map for data imputation and correction in surveys. *Neural Computing and Applications*, 10(4):300–310, 2002. DOI: 10.1007/s005210200002 20

R. Fink, J. Huang, and D. Olteanu. Anytime approximation in probabilistic databases. *The VLDB Journal*, 22(6):823–848, 2013. DOI: 10.1007/s00778-013-0310-5 77

A. Folch-Fortuny, F. Arteaga, and A. Ferrer. Missing data imputation toolbox for MATLAB. *Chemometrics and Intelligent Laboratory Systems*, 154:93–100, 2016. DOI: 10.1016/j.chemolab.2016.03.019 23

M. J. Franklin, D. Kossmann, T. Kraska, S. Ramesh, and R. Xin. CrowdDB: Answering queries with crowdsourcing. In *SIGMOD*, pages 61–72, 2011. DOI: 10.1145/1989323.1989331 11, 22, 66

T. Friedman and M. Smith. *Measuring the business value of data quality*. Gartner, 2011. 3

J. Gao, X. Liu, B. C. Ooi, H. Wang, and G. Chen. An online cost sensitive decision-making method in crowdsourcing systems. In *SIGMOD*, pages 217–228, 2013. DOI: 10.1145/2463676.2465307 11

Y. Gao, X. Miao, H. Cui, G. Chen, and Q. Li. Processing k-skyband, constrained skyline, and group-by skyline queries on incomplete data. *Expert Systems with Applications*, 41(10): 4959–4974, 2014. DOI: 10.1016/j.eswa.2014.02.033 9, 55

Y. Gao, Q. Liu, B. Zheng, L. Mou, G. Chen, and Q. Li. On processing reverse k-skyband and ranked reverse skyline queries. *Information Sciences*, 293:11–34, 2015. DOI: 10.1016/j.ins.2014.08.052 30

J. C. F. García, D. Kalenatic, and C. A. L. Bello. Missing data imputation in multivariate data by evolutionary algorithms. *Computers in Human Behavior*, 27(5):1468–1474, 2011. DOI: 10.1016/j.chb.2010.06.026 22

P. J. García-Laencina, J.-L. Sancho-Gómez, A. R. Figueiras-Vidal, and M. Verleysen. K nearest neighbors with mutual information for simultaneous classification and missing data imputation. *Neurocomputing*, 72(7):1483–1493, 2009. DOI: 10.1016/j.neucom.2008.11.026 27

P. J. García-Laencina, J.-L. Sancho-Gómez, and A. R. Figueiras-Vidal. Pattern classification with missing data: A review. *Neural Computing and Applications*, 19(2):263–282, 2010. DOI: 10.1007/s00521-009-0295-6 18, 19

C. Gautam and V. Ravi. Evolving clustering based data imputation. In *Proc. of International Conference on Circuit, Power and Computing Technologies*, pages 1763–1769, IEEE, 2014. DOI: 10.1109/iccpct.2014.7054988 22

C. Gautam and V. Ravi. Data imputation via evolutionary computation, clustering and a neural network. *Neurocomputing*, 156:134–142, 2015. DOI: 10.1016/j.neucom.2014.12.073 22

P. Godfrey, R. Shipley, and J. Gryz. Maximal vector computation in large data sets. In *VLDB*, pages 229–240, VLDB Endowment, 2005. 29

C. P. Gomes, A. Sabharwal, and B. Selman. Model counting. 2008. 73

J. Graham. *Missing Data: Analysis and Design*. Statistics for Social and Behavioral Sciences, Springer, 2012. DOI: 10.1007/978-1-4614-4018-5. 3

S. Greco, C. Molinaro, and F. Spezzano. Incomplete data and data dependencies in relational databases. *Synthesis Lectures on Data Management*, 4(5):1–123, 2012. DOI: 10.2200/s00435ed1v01y201207dtm029 3

T. J. Green and V. Tannen. Models for incomplete and probabilistic information. In *EDBT*, pages 278–296, 2006. DOI: 10.1007/11896548_24 69

J. W. Grzymala-Busse. Rough set strategies to data with missing attribute values. In *Foundations and Novel Approaches in Data Mining*, pages 197–212, Springer, 2006. DOI: 10.1007/11539827_11 23

J. W. Grzymala-Busse and A. Y. Wang. Modified algorithms LEM1 and LEM2 for rule induction from data with missing attribute values. In *Proc. of the 5th International Workshop on Rough Sets and Soft Computing at the 3rd Joint Conference on Information Sciences*, pages 69–72, 1997. 23

Y. Gulzar, A. A. Alwan, N. Salleh, and I. F. Al Shaikhli. Processing skyline queries in incomplete database: Issues, challenges and future trends. *Journal of Computer Science*, preprint, 2017. DOI: 10.3844/jcssp.2017.647.658 8

S. Guo, A. Parameswaran, and H. Garcia-Molina. So who won?: Dynamic max discovery with the crowd. In *SIGMOD*, pages 385–396, 2012. DOI: 10.1145/2213836.2213880 12

R. Gupta and S. Sarawagi. Answering table augmentation queries from unstructured lists on the Web. *PVLDB*, 2(1):289–300, 2009. DOI: 10.14778/1687627.1687661 22

A. Guttman. R-trees: A dynamic index structure for spatial searching, *ACM*, vol. 14, 1984. DOI: 10.1145/602264.602266 4, 14, 26

P. Haghani, S. Michel, and K. Aberer. Evaluating top-k queries over incomplete data streams. In *CIKM*, pages 877–886, 2009. DOI: 10.1145/1645953.1646064 10, 14, 66

X. Han, J. Li, and H. Gao. TDEP: Efficiently processing top-k dominating query on massive data. *Knowledge and Information Systems*, 43(3):689–718, 2015. DOI: 10.1007/s10115-013-0728-5 32

H. R. Hassanzadeh, J. H. Phan, and M. D. Wang. A semi-supervised method for predicting cancer survival using incomplete clinical data. In *Proc. of International Conference of the IEEE Engineering in Medicine and Biology Society*, pages 210–213, 2015. DOI: 10.1109/embc.2015.7318337 3

G. R. Hjaltason and H. Samet. Ranking in spatial databases. In *International Symposium on Spatial Databases*, pages 83–95, Springer, 1995. DOI: 10.1007/3-540-60159-7_6 26

G. R. Hjaltason and H. Samet. Distance browsing in spatial databases. *ACM Transactions on Database Systems*, 24(2):265–318, 1999. DOI: 10.1145/320248.320255 25, 26

J. Huang, L. Antova, C. Koch, and D. Olteanu. MayBMS: A probabilistic database management system. In *SIGMOD*, pages 1071–1074, ACM, 2009. DOI: 10.1145/1559845.1559984 12

N. Q. V. Hung, D. C. Thang, M. Weidlich, and K. Aberer. Minimizing efforts in validating crowd answers. In *SIGMOD*, pages 999–1014, ACM, 2015. DOI: 10.1145/2723372.2723731 22

I. F. Ilyas and M. A. Soliman. Probabilistic ranking techniques in relational databases. *Synthesis Lectures on Data Management*, 3(1):1–71, 2011. DOI: 10.2200/s00344ed1v01y201103dtm014 4

T. Imieliński and W. Lipski Jr. Incomplete information in relational databases. *Journal of the ACM*, 31(4):761–791, 1984. DOI: 10.1145/1634.1886 3, 17, 67, 69

J. M. Jerez, I. Molina, P. J. García-Laencina, E. Alba, N. Ribelles, M. Martín, and L. Franco. Missing data imputation using statistical and machine learning methods in a real breast cancer problem. *Artificial Intelligence in Medicine*, 50(2):105–115, 2010. DOI: 10.1016/j.artmed.2010.05.002 21

J. R. B. Junior, M. do Carmo Nicoletti, and L. Zhao. An embedded imputation method via attribute-based decision graphs. *Expert Systems with Applications*, 57:159–177, 2016. DOI: 10.1016/j.eswa.2016.03.027 23

S. Kambhampati, G. Wolf, Y. Chen, H. Khatri, B. Chokshi, J. Fan, and U. Nambiar. QUIC: Handling query imprecision and data incompleteness in autonomous databases. In *CIDR*, pages 7–10, 2007. 12

M. E. Khalefa, M. F. Mokbel, and J. J. Levandoski. Skyline query processing for incomplete data. In *ICDE*, pages 556–565, 2008. DOI: 10.1109/icde.2008.4497464 8, 14, 17, 30, 31, 33, 66

K. Kolomvatsos, C. Anagnostopoulos, and S. Hadjiefthymiades. A time optimized scheme for top-k list maintenance over incomplete data streams. *Information Sciences*, 311:59–73, 2015. DOI: 10.1016/j.ins.2015.03.035 11

M. Kontaki, A. N. Papadopoulos, and Y. Manolopoulos. Continuous top-k dominating queries. *IEEE Transactions on Knowledge Data Engineering*, 24(5):840–853, 2012. DOI: 10.1109/tkde.2011.43 32

F. Korn and S. Muthukrishnan. Influence sets based on reverse nearest neighbor queries. In *ACM Sigmod Record*, vol. 29, pages 201–212, ACM, 2000. DOI: 10.1145/335191.335415 26

D. Kossmann, F. Ramsak, and S. Rost. Shooting stars in the sky: An online algorithm for skyline queries. In *VLDB*, pages 275–286, VLDB Endowment, 2002. 29

H.-P. Kriegel, P. Kunath, and M. Renz. Probabilistic nearest-neighbor query on uncertain objects. *Advances in Databases: Concepts, Systems and Applications*, pages 337–348, 2007. DOI: 10.1007/978-3-540-71703-4_30 26, 27

M. Krishna and V. Ravi. Particle swarm optimization and covariance matrix based data imputation. In *Proc. of Computational Intelligence and Computing Research*, pages 1–6, IEEE, 2013. DOI: 10.1109/iccic.2013.6724232 22

T. Kuosmanen and T. Post. Measuring economic efficiency with incomplete price information: With an application to European commercial banks. *European Journal of Operational Research*, 134(1):43–58, 2001. DOI: 10.1016/s0377-2217(00)00237-x 2

T. M. N. Le, J. Cao, and Z. He. Answering skyline queries on probabilistic data using the dominance of probabilistic skyline tuples. *Information Sciences*, 340:58–85, 2016. DOI: 10.1016/j.ins.2016.01.016 29

J. Lee, H. Im, and G.-w. You. Optimizing skyline queries over incomplete data. *Information Sciences*, 361:14–28, 2016a. DOI: 10.1016/j.ins.2016.04.048 8

J. Lee, D. Lee, and S.-W. Kim. Crowdsky: Skyline computation with crowdsourcing. In *EDBT*, pages 125–136, 2016b. DOI: 10.5441/002/edbt.2016.14. 31

J. Lee, D. Lee, and S.-W. Hwang. CrowdK: Answering top-k queries with crowdsourcing. *Information Sciences*, 399:98–120, 2017. DOI: 10.1016/j.ins.2017.03.010 12

K. C. Lee, W.-C. Lee, B. Zheng, H. Li, and Y. Tian. Z-SKY: An efficient skyline query processing framework based on Z-order. *VLDB Journal*, 19(3):333–362, 2010. DOI: 10.1007/s00778-009-0166-x 29, 30

C. Leke, T. Marwala, and S. Paul. Proposition of a theoretical model for missing data imputation using deep learning and evolutionary algorithms, arXiv preprint. 2015. 23

G. Li, J. Wang, Y. Zheng, and M. Franklin. Crowdsourced data management: A survey. *IEEE Transactions on Knowledge Data Engineering*, 28(9):2296–2319, 2016. DOI: 10.1109/icde.2017.26 12

G. Li, Y. Zheng, J. Fan, J. Wang, and R. Cheng. Crowdsourced data management: Overview and challenges. In *Proc. of the ACM International Conference on Management of Data*, pages 1711–1716, ACM, 2017a. DOI: 10.1145/3035918.3054776 12

Y. Li, F. Li, K. Yi, B. Yao, and M. Wang. Flexible aggregate similarity search. In *SIGMOD*, pages 1009–1020, ACM, 2011. DOI: 10.1145/1989323.1989429 26

Y. Li, N. M. Kou, H. Wang, Z. Gong, et al. A confidence-aware top-k query processing toolkit on crowdsourcing. *PVLDB*, 10(12):1909–1912, 2017b. DOI: 10.14778/3137765.3137806 12

Z. Li, M. A. Sharaf, L. Sitbon, S. Sadiq, M. Indulska, and X. Zhou. A web-based approach to data imputation. *World Wide Web*, 17(5):873–897, 2014. DOI: 10.1007/s11280-013-0263-z 22

Z. Li, L. Qin, H. Cheng, X. Zhang, and X. Zhou. TRIP: An interactive retrieving-inferring data imputation approach. *IEEE Transactions on Knowledge Data Engineering*, 27(9):2550–2563, 2015. DOI: 10.1109/icde.2016.7498375 22

X. Lian and L. Chen. Monochromatic and bichromatic reverse skyline search over uncertain databases. In *SIGMOD*, pages 213–226, 2008. DOI: 10.1145/1376616.1376641 29

X. Lian and L. Chen. Top-k dominating queries in uncertain databases. In *EDBT*, pages 660–671, ACM, 2009. DOI: 10.1145/1516360.1516437 32

X. Lian and L. Chen. Probabilistic top-k dominating queries in uncertain databases. *Information Sciences*, 226:23–46, 2013. DOI: 10.1016/j.ins.2012.10.020 32

L. Libkin. Incomplete information and certain answers in general data models. In *PODS*, pages 59–70, ACM, 2011. DOI: 10.1145/1989284.1989294 3

L. Libkin. Incomplete data: What went wrong, and how to fix it. In *PODS*, pages 1–13, 2014. DOI: 10.1145/2594538.2594561 3

L. Libkin. Certain answers as objects and knowledge. *Artificial Intelligence*, 232:1–19, 2016a. DOI: 10.1016/j.artint.2015.11.004 3

L. Libkin. SQL's three-valued logic and certain answers. *ACM Transactions on Database Systems (TODS)*, 41(1):1, 2016b. DOI: 10.1145/2877206 3

A. W.-C. Liew, N.-F. Law, and H. Yan. Missing value imputation for gene expression data: Computational techniques to recover missing data from available information. *Briefings in Bioinformatics*, 12(5):498–513, 2011. DOI: 10.1093/bib/bbq080 2

X. Lin, Y. Yuan, Q. Zhang, and Y. Zhang. Selecting stars: The k most representative skyline operator. In *ICDE*, pages 86–95, IEEE, 2007. DOI: 10.1109/icde.2007.367854 29

R. J. Little and D. B. Rubin. *Statistical Analysis with Missing Data*, 2nd ed., Wiley, 2002. DOI: 10.1002/9781119013563 25

R. J. Little and D. B. Rubin. *Statistical Analysis with Missing Data*. John Wiley & Sons, 2014. DOI: 10.1002/9781119013563 17, 18

S. Liu, H. Dai, and M. Gan. Information-decomposition-model-based missing value estimation for not missing at random dataset. *International Journal of Machine Learning and Cybernetics*, pages 1–11, 2015. DOI: 10.1007/s13042-015-0354-5 23

X. Liu, D.-N. Yang, M. Ye, and W.-C. Lee. U-skyline: A new skyline query for uncertain databases. *IEEE Transactions on Knowledge Data Engineering*, 25(4):945–960, 2013. DOI: 10.1109/tkde.2012.33 29

F. Lobato, C. Sales, I. Araujo, V. Tadaiesky, L. Dias, L. Ramos, and A. Santana. Multi-objective genetic algorithm for missing data imputation. *Pattern Recognition Letters*, 68:126–131, 2015. DOI: 10.1016/j.patrec.2015.08.023 21, 22

C. Lofi, K. El Maarry, and W.-T. Balke. Skyline queries in crowd-enabled databases. In *EDBT*, pages 465–476, 2013a. DOI: 10.1145/2452376.2452431 14, 31

C. Lofi, K. El Maarry, and W.-T. Balke. Skyline queries over incomplete data-error models for focused crowd-sourcing. In *Proc. of International Conference on Conceptual Modeling*, pages 298–312, Springer, 2013b. DOI: 10.1007/978-3-642-41924-9_25 31

Z. Ma, K. Zhang, S. Wang, and C. Yu. A double-index-based k-dominant skyline algorithm for incomplete data stream. In *ICSESS*, pages 750–753, 2013. DOI: 10.1109/icsess.2013.6615414 11

B. F. Manly. *Multivariate Statistical Methods: A Primer*. CRC Press, 1994. DOI: 10.2307/2531558 19

V. Mansinghka, R. Tibbetts, J. Baxter, P. Shafto, and B. Eaves. BayesDB: A probabilistic programming system for querying the probable implications of data. *ArXiv Preprint ArXiv:1512.05006*, 2015. 20

A. Marcus, E. Wu, D. Karger, S. Madden, and R. Miller. Human-powered sorts and joins. *PVLDB*, 5(1):13–24, 2011a. DOI: 10.14778/2047485.2047487 11

A. Marcus, E. Wu, D. R. Karger, S. Madden, and R. C. Miller. Crowdsourced databases: Query processing with people. In *CIDR*, 2011b. 11

X. Miao, Y. Gao, L. Chen, G. Chen, Q. Li, and T. Jiang. On efficient k-skyband query processing over incomplete data. In *DASFAA*, pages 424–439, 2013. DOI: 10.1007/978-3-642-37487-6_32 9

X. Miao, Y. Gao, G. Chen, H. Cui, C. Guo, and W. Pan. SI²P: A restaurant recommendation system using preference queries over incomplete information. *PVLDB*, 9(13):1509–1512, 2016a. http://www.vldb.org/pvldb/vol9/p1509-miao.pdf DOI: 10.14778/3007263.3007296 14, 35

X. Miao, Y. Gao, G. Chen, and T. Zhang. k-dominant skyline queries on incomplete data. *Information Sciences*, 367:990–1011, 2016b. DOI: 10.1016/j.ins.2016.07.034 9

X. Miao, Y. Gao, G. Chen, B. Zheng, and H. Cui. Processing incomplete k nearest neighbor search. *IEEE Transactions on Fuzzy Systems*, 24(6):1349–1363, 2016c. DOI: 10.1109/TFUZZ.2016.2516562. 66

X. Miao, Y. Gao, B. Zheng, G. Chen, and H. Cui. Top-k dominating queries on incomplete data. *IEEE Transactions on Knowledge and Data Engineering*, 28(1):252–266, 2016d. DOI: 10.1109/icde.2016.7498394 30, 66

E. Miyama and S. Managi. Global environmental emissions estimate: Application of multiple imputation. *Environmental Economics and Policy Studies*, 16(2):115–135, 2014. DOI: 10.1007/s10018-014-0080-3 3

F. V. Nelwamondo, D. Golding, and T. Marwala. A dynamic programming approach to missing data estimation using neural networks. *Information Sciences*, 237:49–58, 2013. DOI: 10.1016/j.ins.2009.10.008 23

C. Nieke, U. Güntzer, and W.-T. Balke. Topcrowd. In *Proc. of International Conference on Conceptual Modeling*, pages 122–135, Springer, 2014. DOI: 10.1007/978-3-319-12206-9_10 12

S. Nutanong, E. Tanin, and R. Zhang. Incremental evaluation of visible nearest neighbor queries. *IEEE Transactions on Knowledge Data Engineering*, 22(5):665, 2010. DOI: 10.1109/tkde.2009.158 26

B. C. Ooi, C. H. Goh, and K.-L. Tan. Fast high-dimensional data search in incomplete databases. In *PVLDB*, pages 357–367, 1998. 4

R. Pan, T. Yang, J. Cao, K. Lu, and Z. Zhang. Missing data imputation by *k* nearest neighbors based on grey relational structure and mutual information. *Applied Intelligence*, 43(3):614–632, 2015. DOI: 10.1007/s10489-015-0666-x 23

D. Papadias, Y. Tao, G. Fu, and B. Seeger. Progressive skyline computation in database systems. *ACM Transactions on Database Systems*, 30(1):41–82, 2005a. DOI: 10.1145/1061318.1061320 29, 32

D. Papadias, Y. Tao, K. Mouratidis, and C. K. Hui. Aggregate nearest neighbor queries in spatial databases. *ACM Transactions on Database Systems*, 30(2):529–576, 2005b. DOI: 10.1145/1071610.1071616 26

A. Papadopoulos and Y. Manolopoulos. Performance of nearest neighbor queries in R-trees. *ICDT*, pages 394–408, 1997. DOI: 10.1007/3-540-62222-5_59 25, 26

A. G. Parameswaran, H. Garcia-Molina, H. Park, N. Polyzotis, A. Ramesh, and J. Widom. Crowdscreen: Algorithms for filtering data with humans. In *SIGMOD*, pages 361–372, ACM, 2012a. DOI: 10.1145/2213836.2213878 11

A. G. Parameswaran, H. Park, H. Garcia-Molina, N. Polyzotis, and J. Widom. Deco: Declarative crowdsourcing. In *CIKM*, pages 1203–1212, ACM, 2012b. DOI: 10.1145/2396761.2398421 11

J. Pei, B. Jiang, X. Lin, and Y. Yuan. Probabilistic skylines on uncertain data. In *VLDB*, pages 15–26, 2007. 29

A. Plaia and A. L. Bondì. Single imputation method of missing values in environmental pollution data sets. *Atmospheric Environment*, 40(38):7316–7330, 2006. DOI: 10.1016/j.atmosenv.2006.06.040 3

A. K. Pujari, V. R. Kagita, A. Garg, and V. Padmanabhan. Efficient computation for probabilistic skyline over uncertain preferences. *Information Sciences*, 324:146–162, 2015. DOI: 10.1016/j.ins.2015.06.041 30

B. Qarabaqi and M. Riedewald. User-driven refinement of imprecise queries. In *ICDE*, pages 916–927, IEEE, 2014. DOI: 10.1109/icde.2014.6816711 84

R. Raghunathan, S. De, and S. Kambhampati. Bayesian networks for supporting query processing over incomplete autonomous databases. *Journal of Intelligent Information Systems*, 42 (3):595–618, 2014. DOI: 10.1007/s10844-013-0277-0 12

N. Roussopoulos, S. Kelley, and F. Vincent. Nearest neighbor queries. In *ACM SIGMOD Record*, vol. 24, pages 71–79, ACM, 1995. DOI: 10.1145/568271.223794 25, 26

D. B. Rubin. *Multiple Imputation for Nonresponse in Surveys*, vol. 81, John Wiley & Sons, 2004. DOI: 10.1002/9780470316696 19

D. Sacharidis, P. Bouros, and T. Sellis. Caching dynamic skyline queries. In *SSDBM*, pages 455–472, Springer, 2008. DOI: 10.1007/978-3-540-69497-7_29 41

T. Samad and S. A. Harp. Self-organization with partial data. *Network: Computation in Neural Systems*, 2009. DOI: 10.1088/0954-898x_3_2_008 20

T. Sang, P. Beame, and H. Kautz. Heuristics for fast exact model counting. In *Theory and Applications of Satisfiability Testing*, pages 226–240, Springer, 2005. DOI: 10.1007/11499107_17 73

B. Santoso and G. Chiu. Close dominance graph: An efficient framework for answering continuous top-k dominating queries. *IEEE Transactions on Knowledge Data Engineering*, 26(8): 1853–1865, 2014. DOI: 10.1109/tkde.2013.172 32

P. Schmitt, J. Mandel, and M. Guedj. A comparison of six methods for missing data imputation. *Journal of Biometrics and Biostatistics*, 2015. DOI: 10.4172/2155-6180.1000224 21

T. Schneider. Analysis of incomplete climate data: Estimation of mean values and covariance matrices and imputation of missing values. *Journal of Climate*, 14(5):853–871, 2001. DOI: 10.1175/1520-0442(2001)014<0853:aoicde>2.0.co;2 3

C. Sheng and Y. Tao. Worst-case I/O-efficient skyline algorithms. *ACM Transactions on Database Systems*, 37(4):26, 2012. DOI: 10.1145/2389241.2389245 29

M. A. Soliman, I. F. Ilyas, and S. Ben-David. Supporting ranking queries on uncertain and incomplete data. *VLDB Journal*, 19(4):477–501, 2010. DOI: 10.1007/s00778-009-0176-8 66

S. Song and L. Chen. Differential dependencies: Reasoning and discovery. *ACM Transactions on Database Systems*, 36(3):16, 2011. DOI: 10.1145/2000824.2000826 22

S. Song, A. Zhang, L. Chen, and J. Wang. Enriching data imputation with extensive similarity neighbors. *PVLDB*, 8(11):1286–1297, 2015. DOI: 10.14778/2809974.2809989 22

K.-L. Tan, P.-K. Eng, and B. C. Ooi. Efficient progressive skyline computation. In *VLDB*, pages 301–310, 2001. 29, 41

Y. Tao, R. Cheng, X. Xiao, W. K. Ngai, B. Kao, and S. Prabhakar. Indexing multi-dimensional uncertain data with arbitrary probability density functions. In *VLDB*, pages 922–933, VLDB Endowment, 2005. 27

Y. Tao, D. Papadias, X. Lian, and X. Xiao. Multidimensional reverse KNN search. *VLDB Journal*, 16(3):293–316, 2007. DOI: 10.1007/s00778-005-0168-2 26

Y. Tao, L. Ding, X. Lin, and J. Pei. Distance-based representative skyline. In *ICDE*, pages 892–903, IEEE, 2009. DOI: 10.1109/icde.2009.84 29

M. Templ, A. Alfons, and P. Filzmoser. Exploring incomplete data using visualization techniques. *Advances in Data Analysis and Classification*, 6(1):29–47, 2012. DOI: 10.1007/s11634-011-0102-y 23

C. Thiffault, F. Bacchus, and T. Walsh. Solving non-clausal formulas with DPLL search. *Principles and Practice of Constraint Programming, (CP)*, pages 663–678, 2004. DOI: 10.1007/978-3-540-30201-8_48 73

E. Tiakas, A. N. Papadopoulos, and Y. Manolopoulos. Progressive processing of subspace dominating queries. *VLDB Journal*, 20(6):921–948, 2011. DOI: 10.1007/s00778-011-0231-0 32

E. Tiakas, G. Valkanas, A. N. Papadopoulos, Y. Manolopoulos, and D. Gunopulos. Metric-based top-*k* dominating queries. In *EDBT*, pages 415–426, 2014. DOI: 10.5441/002/edbt.2014.38. 32

J. Tian, B. Yu, D. Yu, and S. Ma. Missing data analyses: A hybrid multiple imputation algorithm using Gray System Theory and entropy based on clustering. *Applied Intelligence*, 40(2):376–388, 2014. DOI: 10.1007/s10489-013-0469-x 23

B. Trushkowsky, T. Kraska, M. J. Franklin, and P. Sarkar. Crowdsourced enumeration queries. In *ICDE*, pages 673–684, IEEE, 2013. DOI: 10.1109/icde.2013.6544865 11, 22

B. Twala, M. Cartwright, and M. Shepperd. Comparison of various methods for handling incomplete data in software engineering databases. In *ISESE*, IEEE, 2005. DOI: 10.1109/isese.2005.1541819 17, 21

G. Van den Broeck and D. Suciu. Query processing on probabilistic data: A survey. *Foundations and Trends® in Databases*, 7(3-4):197–341, 2017. DOI: 10.1561/1900000052 4

M. M. Van Hulle. Self-organizing maps. In *Handbook of Natural Computing*, pages 585–622, Springer, 2012. DOI: 10.1007/978-3-540-92910-9_19 20

J. Van Hulse and T. M. Khoshgoftaar. Incomplete-case nearest neighbor imputation in software measurement data. *Information Sciences*, 259:596–610, 2014. DOI: 10.1016/j.ins.2010.12.017 27

P. Venetis, H. Garcia-Molina, K. Huang, and N. Polyzotis. Max algorithms in crowdsourcing environments. In *WWW*, pages 989–998, ACM, 2012. DOI: 10.1145/2187836.2187969 12

V. Verroios, P. Lofgren, and H. Garcia-Molina. TDP: An optimal-latency budget allocation strategy for crowdsourced maximum operations. In *SIGMOD*, pages 1047–1062, ACM, 2015. DOI: 10.1145/2723372.2749440 12

J. Wang, T. Kraska, M. J. Franklin, and J. Feng. Crowder: Crowdsourcing entity resolution. *PVLDB*, 5(11):1483–1494, 2012. DOI: 10.14778/2350229.2350263 11

J. Wang, G. Li, T. Kraska, M. J. Franklin, and J. Feng. Leveraging transitive relations for crowd-sourced joins. In *SIGMOD*, pages 229–240, ACM, 2013. DOI: 10.1145/2463676.2465280 11

S. Wang, X. Xiao, and C.-H. Lee. Crowd-based deduplication: An adaptive approach. In *SIGMOD*, pages 1263–1277, ACM, 2015. DOI: 10.1145/2723372.2723739 11

Y. Wang and C. Chen. Grey markov model forecast in economic system under incomplete information and its application on foreign direct investment. In *Proc. of the International Conference on Information Management, Innovation Management and Industrial Engineering*, vol. 2, pages 117–120, IEEE, 2011. DOI: 10.1109/iciii.2011.175 2

J. Widom. Trio: A system for integrated management of data, accuracy, and lineage. *Technical Report*, 2004. 12

G. Wolf, H. Khatri, B. Chokshi, J. Fan, Y. Chen, and S. Kambhampati. Query processing over incomplete autonomous databases. In *PVLDB*, pages 651–662, VLDB Endowment, 2007. DOI: 10.1109/icde.2007.369028 12

G. Wolf, A. Kalavagattu, H. Khatri, R. Balakrishnan, B. Chokshi, J. Fan, Y. Chen, and S. Kambhampati. Query processing over incomplete autonomous databases: Query rewriting using learned data dependencies. *VLDB Journal*, 18(5):1167–1190, 2009. DOI: 10.1007/s00778-009-0155-0 12

K. Wu, E. J. Otoo, and A. Shoshani. Compressing bitmap indexes for faster search operations. In *SSDBM*, pages 99–108, IEEE, 2002. DOI: 10.1109/ssdm.2002.1029710 41, 43

K. Wu, A. Shoshani, and K. Stockinger. Analyses of multi-level and multi-component compressed bitmap indexes. *ACM Transactions Database Systems*, 35(1):2, 2010. DOI: 10.1145/1670243.1670245 41, 43, 65, 71

X. Xie, R. Cheng, M. L. Yiu, L. Sun, and J. Chen. UV-diagram: A Voronoi diagram for uncertain spatial databases. *VLDB Journal*, 22(3):319–344, 2013. DOI: 10.1007/s00778-012-0290-x 26, 27

M. Yakout, K. Ganjam, K. Chakrabarti, and S. Chaudhuri. Infogather: Entity augmentation and attribute discovery by holistic matching with web tables. In *SIGMOD*, pages 97–108, ACM, 2012. DOI: 10.1145/2213836.2213848 22

M. L. Yiu and N. Mamoulis. Efficient processing of top-k dominating queries on multi-dimensional data. In *VLDB*, pages 483–494, VLDB Endowment, 2007. DOI: 10.1007/s11280-015-0340-6 32

M. L. Yiu and N. Mamoulis. Multi-dimensional top-k dominating queries. *VLDB Journal*, 18 (3):695–718, 2009. DOI: 10.1007/s00778-008-0117-y 32

M.-C. Yuen, I. King, and K.-S. Leung. A survey of crowdsourcing systems. In *IEEE International Conference on Privacy, Security, Risk, and Trust, and IEEE International Conference on Social Computing*, pages 766–773, 2011. DOI: 10.1109/passat/socialcom.2011.203 14, 65

M. Zaffalon, K. Wesnes, and O. Petrini. Reliable diagnoses of dementia by the naive credal classifier inferred from incomplete cognitive data. *Artificial Intelligence in Medicine*, 29(1): 61–79, 2003. DOI: 10.1016/s0933-3657(03)00046-0 3

L. Zhan, Y. Zhang, W. Zhang, and X. Lin. Identifying top k dominating objects over uncertain data. In *DASFAA*, pages 388–405, Springer, 2014. DOI: 10.1007/978-3-319-05810-8_26 32

J. Zhang, D. Papadias, K. Mouratidis, and Z. Manli. Query processing in spatial databases containing obstacles. *International Journal of Geographical Information Science*, 19(10):1091–1111, 2005. DOI: 10.1080/13658810500286935 26

K. Zhang, H. Gao, H. Wang, and J. Li. ISSA: Efficient skyline computation for incomplete data. In *DASFAA*, pages 321–328, Springer, 2016a. DOI: 10.1007/978-3-319-32055-7_26 8

K. Zhang, H. Gao, X. Han, Z. Cai, and J. Li. Probabilistic skyline on incomplete data. In *CIKM*, pages 427–436, ACM, 2017. DOI: 10.1145/3132847.3132930 8

P. Zhang, R. Cheng, N. Mamoulis, M. Renz, A. Züfle, Y. Tang, and T. Emrich. Voronoi-based nearest neighbor search for multi-dimensional uncertain databases. In *ICDE*, pages 158–169, IEEE, 2013. DOI: 10.1109/icde.2013.6544822 26, 27

S. Zhang, N. Mamoulis, and D. W. Cheung. Scalable skyline computation using object-based space partitioning. In *SIGMOD*, pages 483–494, ACM, 2009. DOI: 10.1145/1559845.1559897 29, 30

S. Zhang, Z. Jin, and X. Zhu. Missing data imputation by utilizing information within incomplete instances. *Journal of Systems and Software*, 84(3):452–459, 2011. DOI: 10.1016/j.jss.2010.11.887 23

W. Zhang, X. Lin, Y. Zhang, J. Pei, and W. Wang. Threshold-based probabilistic top-k dominating queries. *VLDB Journal*, 19(2):283–305, 2010a. DOI: 10.1007/s00778-009-0162-1 32

X. Zhang, G. Li, and J. Feng. Crowdsourced top-k algorithms: An experimental evaluation. *PVLDB*, 9(8):612–623, 2016b. DOI: 10.14778/2921558.2921559 12

Y. Zhang, W. Zhang, Q. Lin, and X. Lin. Effectively indexing the multi-dimensional uncertain objects for range searching. In *EDBT*, pages 504–515, ACM, 2012. DOI: 10.1145/2247596.2247655 27

Z. Zhang, H. Lu, B. C. Ooi, and A. K. Tung. Understanding the meaning of a shifted sky: A general framework on extending skyline query. *VLDB Journal*, 19(2):181–201, 2010b. DOI: 10.1007/s00778-009-0148-z 8, 29

F. Zhao, G. Das, K.-L. Tan, and A. K. Tung. Call to order: A hierarchical browsing approach to eliciting users' preference. In *SIGMOD*, pages 27–38, 2010. DOI: 10.1145/1807167.1807173 29

C. Zhong, W. Pedrycz, D. Wang, L. Li, and Z. Li. Granular data imputation: A framework of granular computing. *Applied Soft Computing*, 46:307–316, 2016. DOI: 10.1016/j.asoc.2016.05.006 23

X. Zhu, S. Zhang, Z. Jin, Z. Zhang, and Z. Xu. Missing value estimation for mixed-attribute data sets. *IEEE Transactions on Knowledge Data Engineering*, 23(1):110–121, 2011. DOI: 10.1109/tkde.2010.99 21

Authors' Biographies

YUNJUN GAO

Yunjun Gao is a professor at the College of Computer Science, Zhejiang University, China. He received a Ph.D. in computer science from Zhejiang University, China, in 2008. Prior to joining the faculty in 2010, he was a postdoctoral fellow (scientist) at Singapore Management University from 2008–2010, and a visiting scholar or research assistant at Nanyang Technological University, Simon Fraser University, and City University of Hong Kong, respectively. His primary research areas are database, big data management, and AI Interaction with DB Technology. In particular, his current research interests include Data-Driven Machine Learning, Big Graph Data Management and Mining, Geo-Social Data Processing, Data Quality, Metric and Incomplete/Uncertain Data Management, Database Usability, and Spatial and Spatio-Temporal Databases. He has published more than 100 papers in several premium/leading international journals and conferences including TODS, VLDBJ, TKDE, TOIS, SIGMOD, VLDB, ICDE, and SIGIR. He is a member of the ACM and the IEEE, and a senior member of the CCF. He is or was an associate editor of DAPD and IJSSOE, a guest editor of WWWJ, IJDSN, and DSE, and a referee/reviewer of several prestigious journals such as TODS, VLDBJ, TKDE, TMC, and TKDD. He is serving or has served as a PC co-chair, workshop co-chair, publication chair, publicity co-chair, local poster chair, program committee member, or (external) reviewer for various important international conferences such as SIGMOD, VLDB, ICDE, EDBT, CIKM, DASFAA, SIGSPATIAL GIS, APWeb, WAIM, WISE, MDM, among others. He was an awardee/recipient of the NSFC Excellent Young Scholars Program in 2015, the Best Paper Award of APWeb-WAIM 2018, the 2017 CCF Outstanding Doctoral Dissertation Award (Advisor), the 2016 Zhejiang Provincial Outstanding Master's Dissertation Award (Advisor), the First Prize of the Ministry of Education Science and Technology Progress Award (2016), the Nomination of the Best Paper of SIGMOD 2015, one of the Best Papers of ICDE 2015, and the First Prize of Zhejiang Province Science and Technology Award (2011).

XIAOYE MIAO

Xiaoye Miao is a Postdoctoral Fellow at the Department of Computer Science, City University of Hong Kong, China. She received a Ph.D. in computer science from Zhejiang University, China in 2017 and received a B.S. from the College of Computer Science at Xi'an Jiaotong University, China, in 2012. Her research interests include Incomplete/Uncertain Data Management, Graph Data Management, Data Pricing, and Data Cleaning. She has published more than 15 papers in several premium/leading international journals and conferences including VLDBJ, TKDE, VLDB, and ICDE. She is serving or has served as an (external) reviewer for a variety of important international journals and conferences such as VLDB Journal, TKDE, Information Sciences, WWW Journal, JCST, VLDB, ICDE, DASFAA, SIGSPATIAL GIS, APWeb, WAIM, DEXA, among others.